Communities of Practice in Higher Education

Drawing on research and practice, this key text provides a rich, detailed, and accessible guide to Communities of Practice (CoPs) theory and how to implement it within higher education. It takes a detailed look at how the theory is constructed, the research that it rests on, and the ways that it has been used and can be used in the future.

Beginning by introducing CoP theory and the theory of learning that accompanies it, this book provides empirical examples of CoP research to illustrate how CoPs form and work within higher education. It also explores how different CoPs work together and can learn from each other. The key topics explored in the book allow the reader to critically understand how CoP theory can be used in higher education to enhance an understanding of how students, staff, and organisations learn.

Ideal reading for those researching higher education practices or undertaking higher education teaching qualifications as well as those currently teaching, this book provides a research-led and critical discussion of the current state of CoP-informed research into learning, teaching, and assessment practices alongside and interleaved with an exploration of how this same approach can be utilised for informing research.

Jonathan Tummons is Professor of Education at Durham University, UK.

Communities of Practice in Higher Education

Learning, Teaching, and Research

Jonathan Tummons

LONDON AND NEW YORK

Designed cover image: Getty Images

First published 2025
by Routledge
4 Park Square, Milton Park, Abingdon, Oxon OX14 4RN

and by Routledge
605 Third Avenue, New York, NY 10158

Routledge is an imprint of the Taylor & Francis Group, an informa business

© 2025 Jonathan Tummons

The right of Jonathan Tummons to be identified as author of this work has been asserted in accordance with sections 77 and 78 of the Copyright, Designs and Patents Act 1988.

All rights reserved. No part of this book may be reprinted or reproduced or utilised in any form or by any electronic, mechanical, or other means, now known or hereafter invented, including photocopying and recording, or in any information storage or retrieval system, without permission in writing from the publishers.

Trademark notice: Product or corporate names may be trademarks or registered trademarks, and are used only for identification and explanation without intent to infringe.

British Library Cataloguing-in-Publication Data
A catalogue record for this book is available from the British Library

ISBN: 978-1-032-53457-2 (hbk)
ISBN: 978-1-032-53458-9 (pbk)
ISBN: 978-1-003-41210-6 (ebk)

DOI: 10.4324/9781003412106

Typeset in Galliard
by KnowledgeWorks Global Ltd.

Contents

Acknowledgements — *vi*
Introduction — *vii*

1 What Is a Community of Practice? — 1

2 Where Is the Learning in a Community of Practice, and How Does It Happen? — 18

3 Communities of Practice in Higher Education: What Can We Learn from the Research? — 35

4 Setting Up a Learning Architecture — 52

5 Communities of Practice: Expansions and Limitations — 68

6 Constellations, Brokers, and Boundaries: How Communities of Practice Learn from and Work with Each Other — 84

7 Assessment Within a Community of Practice — 98

8 Research and Communities of Practices — 115

Index — *129*

Acknowledgements

Thanks are due to Routledge for taking this book on and then being patient with me as the vicissitudes of everyday life saw fit to play havoc with my writing time. Thank you to Sarah Hyde and to Lauren Redhead – I'm really grateful.

My mother, who always used to read everything that I wrote, passed away a few years ago. And so it fell to my father to receive my spare author copies of my books and articles, which he would steel himself to read but never quite manage to finish. But that was okay. My father passed away as I was writing this book, so I am not sure who to send those spare copies to now, but this is for him anyway. And for my mother as well: she would have had great fun teasing me about the long words.

Introduction

The term *Community of Practice* was first introduced in a slim book published in 1991 and then written about much more extensively in a further book published seven years later by one of the authors of the first one. Since then, the idea of communities of practice as places for learning, development, knowledge transfer, and so forth has travelled across many countries and been used to explore a sometimes bewildering array of activities. Higher education is just one such area of activity.

The eight chapters in this book have been arranged in a particular sequence, but I have provided some markers to allow for navigation around the text as a whole where necessary. The ideas that made up CoP theory are not entirely suitable for laying out in a line, and so I have done some judicious signposting to help the links across the chapters become clear. There is some academic jargon, but not too much, and I am not apologetic – lots of things have a specialist jargon attached to them. Key terms from CoP theory are explained throughout and from time to time other key theories from other areas of research literature are drawn on. References for further reading (these are by no means exhaustive and more reflect my own preferences in terms of engagement with the literature than any systematic synthesis) will provide sustenance for those who wish to travel onwards. If more signposts or maps through the CoP terrain are needed, then please feel free to send me an email.

Chapter 1

What Is a Community of Practice?

Introduction

In this chapter, I introduce the concept of the Community of Practice. As we proceed through the book as a whole, further ideas will be introduced that will enrich our understanding of Communities of Practice as well as contextualise our understanding of them within the broader field of higher education. For now, I am going to provide a brief discussion of some of the key tenets of Communities of Practice theory as an introduction to exploring the ways in which the theory can be used to make sense of the stuff that happens in universities: the ways that students learn, the ways that staff learn (and this might not only include academic staff but also administrative staff, as we shall see, although it is the work done by academic staff and by students that will be our prime focus), and the ways that the practices of academic research can be understood. In this way, I shall signpost the main themes of the subsequent chapters of this book and also briefly refer to the theoretical and empirical foundations of the book as a whole.

What Is a Community of Practice?

For some readers of this book, the term "Community of Practice" (from this point onwards frequently abbreviated to CoP) is entirely new. For others, it will be a term that is more or less familiar – a concept or theory (we will consider whether there is a difference between these at a later point) that has been encountered in a staff development workshop, an academic paper, or a research seminar. It is a term that gets applied to describe all kinds of gatherings or collections of people – but oftentimes with insufficient detail and without due care for the insights that the theory can provide us with. It is a concept that can, when used carefully and critically, allow us to interrogate learning – here understood as a social and cultural practice – in all kinds of interesting and useful ways. Done well, an account informed by CoP theory of the learning that happens within university departments or research groups can help us think about how to best establish the social relations of our workplaces (that is to say, our faculty buildings, our laboratories, or our seminar rooms). Such an account can also help us think about the materials and resources that we use in our teaching, the ways in which our research informs our teaching, and the ways in which we come to know about how our universities and departments work and what they do.

So what actually *is* a CoP? Simply put, a CoP is a particular kind of social formation, a clustering of people and material stuff in specific places. All of the people who are members of a CoP are involved in the doing of a particular series of identifiable and defined activities or practices, the doing of which has and will continue to require different episodes or periods of learning. People will have to learn to do the things that the CoP is all about, how to use any required tools and resources, and how to talk and/or write about what they are doing in the manner appropriate to the things they are doing. Some people will want to learn about everything, but other people will be perfectly content to only learn a few things and to ignore others – and some CoPs will allow such flexibility, whereas others may not. Sometimes, however, people will want to learn some particular stuff and are stopped from doing so. The people who are in the CoP might also have to learn about or talk/write about stuff that at first look doesn't seem to be about what goes on in their CoP at all, but is nonetheless necessary. Sometimes, people from one CoP might need to work very closely with people in another CoP. At other times, CoPs keep their distance from each other. Oftentimes, the people within a CoP might have to change what they do and, therefore, what and how they learn things, how they talk about them, how they use their resources, and so forth. Sometimes such changes can be rapid and at other times they might be slow, or even resisted.

CoPs are everywhere, and we are all members of lots of different ones: sometimes we might be highly expert, even important community members. At other times, we might only ever be on the fringes of the CoP. Sometimes we actively seek out membership of new communities, and at other times we might not even be aware that we are members. As people in the world, we engage in all kinds of activities or practices as part of our everyday lives: at work, at play, with families and/or with friends, with people who we hardly know, and with people who we share spaces with on a more or less temporary basis. In order to take part in these practices, we come together in CoPs so that we can talk to each other, share tools and materials, and, most importantly, learn more about what is being done and why. It is sometimes straightforward to work out who might be a member of a particular community, perhaps on account of the clothes that they wear, the tools or objects that they use, or the words and phrases that they employ in their writing or their speech. At other times, discerning the membership of a specific CoP may be more opaque.

We need to note two important points before we proceed to the fine-grained details of the conceptual components of CoP theory (which will necessitate some technical language but, as we shall see, such specialist ways of talking/writing about things are a paradigmatic component of *any* Community of Practice). The first important point is that CoP theory rests on a particular way of defining learning, in which learning is understood not as a psychological process but as a social and cultural one – we shall discuss this in Chapter 2. Consequently, one of the arguments that I put forward in this book is that any serious discussion of CoPs which does not, somewhere, refer to the learning that is happening within that same CoP should be treated with caution. If a rationale for not discussing learning is provided, all well and good; if it is lost sight of or ignored, then the reader has to join the dots themselves and this could lead to misunderstanding. The second important point is that there are lots of different kinds of social and cultural formations of people and things that are *not* Communities of Practice. This is important because there are more than a few examples in the research literature of collectives or communities of people that do not on close reading appear to actually be Communities of Practice even though they have been described as such or, if they are, then the explanations lack sufficiently rich and/or persuasive detail. A CoP is a particular kind of community and we need to be precise and exacting in our use of the term. If CoP theory is going to maintain its explanatory potential – if it is going to continue to be able to provide meaningful insights into the social phenomena that we are interested in unpacking – then it needs to be used properly and respectfully: it needs to be used well. As such, we need to resist labelling something as being a CoP until we are quite certain that what we are interested in really is one.

Some Brief Notes on the History of a Theory

The Community of Practice framework was first posited in a book published in 1991 called *Situated Learning: Legitimate Peripheral Participation*, written by Jean Lave and Etienne Wenger. Jean Lave, who has now retired, was a social anthropologist at the University of California, and Etienne Wenger, who now works as an independent researcher and consultant, had been a doctoral student who had completed his research a year earlier. The empirical examples of CoPs discussed by Lave and Wenger (1991) included apprentice tailors, butchers, and midwives. Seven years later, Wenger published his book *Communities of Practice: learning, meaning and identity*. The empirical examples of CoPs drawn on in this later book included amateur radio operators, recovering alcoholics and office-based computer users, whilst the significant empirical foundations of this work rested on an ethnographic study of a medical insurance claims centre (Wenger, 1998). Lave and Wenger form part of a wider group of writers and researchers based at a number of universities who were interested in thinking about cognition as a social practice, informed in part by the theories of Lev Vygotsky, drawing on anthropological and ethnographic approaches and conducting their fieldwork in a variety of locations ranging from hospitals to blacksmiths' workshops, as well as schools and classrooms. Taken together, this field of scholarship constitutes a now very well-established body of work generally referred to as sociocultural studies of learning and education, sometimes described in terms of a "social turn" (Cole et al., 1997; Lave, 1988, 2011; Nunes et al., 1993; Rogoff, 2003; Rogoff & Lave, 1984; Wertsch et al., 1995).

The main focus of Lave and Wenger's work was not the Community of Practice *per se*, but the exposition of a particular sociocultural theory of learning – Legitimate Peripheral Participation (I return to this in the following chapter). At that point in time, Lave and Wenger defined a CoP in only a cursory manner, as being "largely an intuitive notion, which serves a purpose here but which requires a more rigorous treatment" (Lave & Wenger, 1991, p. 42). Their main focus was on apprenticeship models of learning that in turn could contribute to the generation of a more broadly applicable model of learning as a social practice. Wenger (1998), in his later book, provided the more rigorous treatment that the earlier book called for, through constructing a detailed framework that described and explored what CoPs are, how they are constituted, how they work, how learning happens within them, how people obtain and then sustain membership of CoPs, and how different CoPs might work together.

Unsurprisingly, Wenger's own ideas have shifted over time. He adopted/ advocated a more top-down and applied approach in a subsequent book, *Cultivating Communities of Practice* (Wenger et al., 2002), which was aimed at business management audiences (Barton & Tusting, 2005) and within which CoP was employed as a managerial tool to facilitate specific kinds of organisational learning as a vehicle for improving productivity and competitiveness (Li et al., 2009), described by Hughes (2007, p. 37) as "the communities of practice consultancy movement". More generally, Lea (2005) has argued that successive iterations of CoP theory have led to a shift away from the CoP as a heuristic framework to being a top-down educational model that has been uncritically taken up by subsequent authors, thereby erasing the rich and critical explanatory potential of the earlier CoP framework.

Across the CoP literature as a whole, there are several different critiques of and also advocates for these two distinct approaches to CoPs, which here I shall refer to (co-opting the labels used by Wenger et al., 2002, p. x) as the academic model and the practitioner model respectively. The academic model, I argue, reflects not only the rich empirical work that underpinned both Lave and Wenger (1991) and Wenger (1998) but also the emergent and organic nature of ethnography more broadly that is echoed in the nature of the CoP model derived from these early works and which, I propose, characterises the empirical bases of those CoP-informed accounts of learning and teaching in higher education that are the more convincing and illuminating. From this standpoint, CoPs are understood as found – not constructed – in all kinds of places and thinking about learning within CoPs provides ways of thinking about the social practices of learning that break down artificial distinctions such as 'formal' and 'informal' learning. At the same time, it is important to note that drawing on this CoP approach to explore the social practices of learning in universities is a far from straightforward process: indeed the opposite is the case, not least as the early work of Lave and Wenger rejects any notion of formal pedagogy or pedagogic discourse (a problem that I shall return to on several occasions in subsequent chapters). This, then, is the iteration of CoP theory that I subscribe to although I am keenly aware of several problematic elements within this approach and I shall address these and other tensions later. And I shall also from time to time refer to work that more or less explicitly draws on the practitioner model. There are a number of researchers and writers who have taken up CoPs as a way of thinking and writing about learning in a wide range of settings encompassing both informal and formal contexts for learning, education, and training. Research relating to higher education has covered topics ranging from assessment (Rømer, 2002) to curriculum reform (Annala & Mäkinen, 2016) and professional development (Arthur, 2016) to academic identity (James, 2007), and this broader body of literature is discussed in more detail in Chapter 3: for the present, it is sufficient simply to acknowledge that the broader field of higher education has been subjected to CoP-informed inquiry and analysis through the use of both the academic and the practitioner models.

Back to Communities of Practice

One of the key tenets of my argument in this book therefore, very much derived from the academic CoP model, is that CoPs in and of themselves cannot be invented: it is not possible for a person or group of people to sit down and make one. CoPs emerge, evolve and change over time – some move quickly and others quite slowly, some get very large and others stay small, and some last a very long time whereas others diminish relatively quickly – but you cannot build one from scratch. But what you can do is create a structure to house the conditions within which a CoP might emerge, and this is referred to as a *learning architecture* (Tummons, 2014, 2018; Wenger, 1998). I discuss this more fully in Chapter 4. Thus, if we are primarily interested in exploring extant CoPs, as opposed to establishing learning architectures to allow for the growth of new ones, then it is a relatively straightforward task to go looking for them. Remembering that not every social or community formation that we might encounter is a CoP, we can explore different social formations (from an ethnographic perspective – that is, through an appropriately extensive process of carefully observing the people and practices that are of interest to us) in order to establish whether or not what we are watching, listening to, perhaps even taking part in ourselves, does actually constitute a CoP.

In order to establish whether or not the practices that we are watching are indeed arranged within a CoP, we need to return to the descriptions provided by Wenger (1998) and specifically to three paradigmatic components that any CoP has. Our first step in benchmarking a CoP, therefore, (and our first step in getting to know some of the constructs that lie behind the metalanguage of CoPs) is to look for these three elements: mutual engagement, joint enterprise, and shared repertoire (Wenger, 1998, pp. 73–85). If you can discern all three of these in whatever context – university department, laboratory group, online course – you are interested in, then you are on the way to providing a rich and worthwhile description of a CoP.

Mutual Engagement

In order to get stuff done within a CoP, the members of that community need to have systems, methods, processes, and so forth in place that will provide opportunities to talk, to practice, to share ideas, to swap notes, help each other out with procedures, show people how to use necessary tools and equipment, and so on. This might happen in different ways: some might prefer face-to-face meetings, whereas others might prefer email. In instances such as these, there won't be a problem so long as the CoP has both methods set up as part of its shared routines or *shared repertoire* (I return to this below); otherwise, members will have to adapt their habits to the ways of doing things required by the CoP or risk not being able to participate either fully and/or correctly (this is discussed in Chapter 2). On other occasions, the structures and cultures of the CoP may change and therefore require members to adopt new patterns or formats for participation. Or it might be the case that not all people will want and/or need particularly frequent opportunities for conversations about, or reading materials that are relevant to, the work being undertaken. Sometimes, this won't matter too much, but at other times people may need to engage in the work of the CoP in ways that they are not so comfortable with, and as such may require help and/or persuasion. All of these ways through which the CoP members interact with each other in the doing of whatever they do is described by Wenger as *mutual engagement*. Mutual engagement might always be done on a face-to-face basis or it might involve talking on the phone as well as face-to-face, or meeting on Zoom or MS Teams, or posting messages online. CoP members do not have to agree with each other all the time nor should they be expected to do so. Things can be adjusted, argued over, tried differently and spoken or even argued about in various ways – all forms of mutual engagement.

Joint Enterprise

Any CoP is always "about" something. Sometimes, whatever it is that is the focus of the work done within the CoP – the mental, physical, or emotional effort that is required to keep the CoP going – can be quite tidily and easily defined, whereas at other times it might take a bit more work to say exactly what it is that the CoP does or is interested and engaged in. Some will have explicit, usually written, rules and regulations whereas others may rely on word of mouth, for example. But whether or not we are interested in a group of medievalists meeting in a seminar room and discussing constructions of gender in the works of Christine de Pizan (a prolific author during the late fourteenth and early fifteenth centuries, born in Italy and later living and working in France) or a group of sociologists who are meeting online and discussing constructions of gender in the works of Judith Butler (a contemporary American philosopher and scholar of queer theory and gender studies), these and every other CoP will have a focus, a topic, a thing that they do. This is referred to as the *joint enterprise* of the community. The joint enterprise of a CoP does not have to be always agreed upon by everyone. That is to say, it is in the doing of the work rather than the work itself that sufficient agreement needs to be found, or negotiated, in such a way that the CoP can keep working. The members of the CoP will always work out amongst themselves what is important and what is not, what needs to be done and what can be left behind, what is working well and what needs improving, and so forth. Consequently, the joint enterprise of any CoP can stretch and/or contract over time, according to both internal and external pressures. New things to do may be adopted or acquired or even forced upon the CoP, and old things may become obsolete, fall into disuse through forgetting, or be forcibly removed from the everyday work of members.

Shared Repertoire

The third piece of the jigsaw (for now) requires us to think about how the mutual engagement and the joint enterprise get accomplished. For example, we know that one of the ways in which a CoP agrees on what it is going to be doing (joint enterprise) is through the members of the Community talking to each other (mutual engagement). But how will they do this talking? By "how" I don't mean to ask whether or not they will be meeting up in real life or deciding to use Zoom or even simply choose to do everything by email – that is the "way" or "method" or "where" of talking, perhaps, but not the "how". Instead, I mean to draw attention to how people in the CoP talk with, or write to, other members of the same CoP through using the particular words, phrases and/or jargon that are specific to that CoP. Any community will always have a specific way of doing things – including talking – that helps speed the work along, and specialised ways of talking are just as useful within the CoP as specialised tools or methods are. Moreover, as we shall see in Chapter 2, it is in the picking up of how to talk (and listen) or how to use the materials and equipment of a CoP that the practice of learning becomes visible. All of these elements – the ways of talking, the machinery, the routines, the tools and artefacts, the folders, the PDF files, the portfolios, and so on – are all gathered together as the *shared repertoire* of any given CoP. Sometimes we can share these with other CoPs (this will be discussed in Chapter 6), and sometimes they are unique to just one CoP, perhaps even jealously guarded. But irrespective of whether or not they are commonplace or rare, highly technical or relatively commonplace, any and all aspects of the shared repertoire of the CoP need to be made available to any and all of the CoP members who might legitimately need to make use of them.

Summing Up: Describing Communities of Practice

- A CoP is a social configuration within which people take part in the doing of specified activities or practices.
- The practices of a CoP have to be learned. Within a CoP, learning is understood as a sociocultural, not psychological, process.
- All CoPs have three core components that can be explored through empirical inquiry: mutual engagement, joint enterprise, and shared repertoire.

Interlude: Careful and Meaningful Use of Theory

Wenger's three-part model based on mutual engagement, joint enterprise, and shared repertoire seems, at first look, to provide us with a helpful – and, crucially, straightforward to operationalise – framework for ascertaining the extent to which a gathering of people who are all engaged in particular shared activities constitutes a CoP. Indeed, it seems to be sufficiently straightforward, even being mindful of the fact of being written for academics rather than practitioners (Wenger et al., 2002, p. x) so as to beg the question: why is it not used more often in those instances from the academic literature when people do indeed describe something as a CoP, before dropping in a reference to Wenger (1998)? Part of the problem may well rest in the employment of questionable citation practices – as is arguably the case in relation to references to situated learning within the research literature (Lang & Canning, 2010).

Perhaps an explanation might lie in the evolution of the CoP framework. As mentioned earlier in the chapter, the development of the concept of the CoP – from a brief outline in Lave and Wenger (1991) to the richer and more detailed model of Wenger (1998) and then to the organisational learning framework of Wenger (2000) and Wenger et al. (2002) – might equally indicate a process of evolution that allows for the greater uptake of CoP-informed research due to the very fact of this increased focus on organisations, irrespective of any arguments about the rather different natures, at an epistemological level, of the academic and practitioner models and of the changing uses that these have been put to over time. Descriptions of this evolving body of ideas tend to map the shift from academic to practitioner models in terms of a shift from heuristic framework for inquiry to an applied model for hands-on application (Lea, 2005). At the same time, other writers have critiqued and/or adapted the CoP model/framework in a variety of ways, ranging from the interposing of differing theoretical/conceptual components (Mutch, 2003) to the expansion of the epistemological basis of any CoP (Amin & Roberts, 2008), and – inevitably – this process of evolution/adaption has itself become an object for inquiry (Tight, 2015). Amidst this increased heterogeneity, it is perhaps unsurprising that different research and writing projects have focussed on different iterations of CoP theory and have used them to a variable degree.

My ongoing explorations with the academic model rest on the alignment of that model with my own approach to empirical research – ethnography – as well as my own perspective, namely that it is this model rather than the practitioner model that generates the more useful lines of inquiry and provides more, and more critical, opportunities for insights into the practices of higher education (Tummons, 2012, 2014, 2018, 2023a). However, a more egregious problem rests in the rigour – or otherwise – of the theory-work that surrounds any account of a CoP. All too often, we find collections of people or groups of practices described as being a "community of practice", without any serious attempt to establish *why* it is so. In cases such as these, we find the phenomenon of poor or uncritical use of theory due to the theoretical frameworks in question being either poorly defined and/or poorly operationalised, sometimes in an attempt to generate claims of "epistemological legitimacy and explanatory commentary" (Thomas, 2007, p. 85), and at other times structuring the research "so much that the outcomes of the research are simply a tautological restating of the theory" (Ashwin, 2009, p. 133). This may seem to have been a rather lengthy way of saying that 'good theory use matters' but it *does* matter and the reasons why, as far as this book is concerned, seem to me to need to be articulated rather than remain at a tacit level. If – as I am going to be arguing throughout – critical but also rich and careful use of CoP theories for our inquiries can generate useful insights into the practices of higher education, then it stands to reason that I need to be clear about what I mean when I talk about good theory use in contrast to "theory talk" (Thomas, 2007).

Back to Communities of Practice – Again

Mutual engagement, joint enterprise and shared repertoire are just three of the several paradigmatic components of a CoP, according to the Wenger (1998) framework that I draw on across this book as a whole. Other concepts that are well represented in the literature include *boundaries*, which might seem pretty self-explanatory but do need some explanation (this will be covered in depth in Chapter 6), and *trajectories*, which are the ways in which the journeys of participation and therefore of learning of the people within a CoP are described (these will be explored in the chapter that follows this one). But the first three – mutual engagement, joint enterprise, shared repertoire – provide enough detail to get us started and to allow us to be sure that when we describe something as a CoP, it really is one. We can now begin to think about the CoPs that we might find in and across universities, even across the sector as a whole, with a satisfactory degree of rigour and accuracy – a first step in the careful and meaningful use of theory that I have advocated for above.

Thinking about these theoretical components in purely abstract terms is of interest to some researchers and some theorists, of course, but the test of any good theory, arguably, is what it helps us do in the "real worlds" of the university, of the faculty, of the research group. How does knowing about mutual engagement, or about boundaries when we get to them, help us make sense of the working lives and practices of academics (early career researchers, professors, recent PhD graduates on fixed-term contracts) who are running seminar programmes, convening meetings within a research group, or preparing a paper for submission to a journal? In a way, the answer to this question is simple. My argument is that knowing about and therefore using CoP theory helps us to interrogate our practices as teachers, as external examiners, as research group leaders, as academics. It enhances our professional knowledge – that is, our ways of knowing about the work that we do. It has benefits for us as individuals, for the universities and/or colleges of higher education within which we work, and for the sector as a whole. It is *not* a quick fix, an easy way to encourage (for example) inclusive practice, or a method of guaranteeing equity of collaboration within a research cluster or of encouraging quality improvement within a department (whatever any of those things might mean). It's a shift in perspective, a framework for seeing and thinking about the work that we do in a slightly different way. CoP theory opens us up to thinking about the ways in which our practice might be more authentic and therefore more meaningful for all of the other people enrolled within this same CoP – our colleagues, our students, and our co-authors.

As we work through the subsequent chapters of this book, we will explore a number of different aspects of working in higher education. Some of them will be familiar to many of us and will be an important element of our working lives, such as assessment and feedback, whilst others will be of relevance to only some areas of provision or curriculum, such as industrial placements. Employment and contractual responsibilities vary as well. Some of us will have programme or module leadership responsibilities or hold other leadership roles within or across our home departments (as I have for some years now), whereas others of us will only have responsibility for teaching and for marking assignments (as was the case for me during my eight years of working on part-time and hourly paid contracts at two different universities in the North of England when I was still a medieval historian). Factors such as these all make a difference to our positions within CoPs – our trajectories – and thus to the nature of our work and learning – our participation – within the different CoPs that we are members of, which might be institutional, within a department, or across a faculty. Whether our membership of these CoPs is *full* or *peripheral* (as we shall discuss in Chapter 2), we can still reflect on and theorise aspects of our work in the broadest sense – our pedagogic practice, our research, the ways we give feedback, the ways we design our materials and resources – through the CoP lens. So, if we do start to look at the work done in universities through a CoP lens (axiomatically, from an ethnographic perspective), beginning with mutual engagement, joint enterprise and shared repertoire, then what might we find?

The Mutual Engagement of Higher Education Communities of Practice

For any CoP to be able to do whatever it is that it is about, different patterns and processes of working together have to be established and then maintained, perhaps changed or revised, and even brought to a close if the circumstances require it. Sometimes, changes to how the members of a CoP do their work can change very quickly due to overwhelming external pressures, such as the "online pivot" necessitated during COVID-19. At other times, patterns of change are more gradual: the mundane example of the university lecture is a good example of something which, notwithstanding various technological refinements and any number of more or less well-informed critiques, has remained remarkably stable in form over a long period of time (Tummons, 2023b). Members may need to come together in order to adhere to a highly structured schedule or may be free to work in a very loose and unstructured manner. Sometimes members will be required to use very particular modes of expression and communication, whereas at other times more fluid forms of communication will be appropriate. The practices of some communities may require tightly specified environments (these might be face-to-face and/or online) that have been mandated by external actors – by different CoPs (and I discuss power relations such as these in Chapter 6) – whereas other practices might be accomplished in any number of places or settings.

As with so many things, the practices of any group or constellation of CoPs are characterised by heterogeneity, but such variety nonetheless encompasses a number of familiar forms of coming together that we can now identify in terms of mutual engagement, the recognition of which in turn helps us to identify the CoPs in question, to draw figurative if not always physical boundaries around them. For example, a group of students brought together within a specific programme of study will have at their disposal various affordances for mutual engagement such as attending lectures and seminars, writing lab reports or designing posters, posting to an online discussion board, sharing and learning about material objects (but we have to remember that these may or may not be compulsory to take part in). A group of biologists may come together to discuss their respective analyses of a series of bagged soil samples. A group of psychologists may all take part in a seminar where they discuss an academic paper that debunks a so-called "neuromyth" such as Dale's Cone of Experience. And a group of anthropologists may all attend a series of lectures for a course called "an introduction to social anthropology".

During pedagogical engagements such as these, the particular roles or standpoints occupied by students on the one hand and academics on the other are thrown into sharp relief. Lecturers write and deliver lectures and students listen to them and sometimes take notes. Students write assignments and lecturers provide feedback and grades. Lecturers write course documents and design programmes of study, effectively selecting those aspects of the subject area with which the students will be able to engage. The different practices taken up by lecturers on the one hand and students on the other are for some researchers so different, that it cannot be the case that they belong to the same CoP (Ashwin, 2009). However, for other researchers, these differences in practice reflect the differing positions of students (as apprentices or newcomers) and academics (as experts or old-timers) within the same CoP (James, 2007).

Doing essays – arguably one of the most routinised aspects of university practice – provides a straightforward example of this problem. It is clearly the case that the practices of academics are different from students when considering essays. Academics set the titles, students write the essays, academics do the marking and write the feedback, and so forth. We might easily see these as distinct practices: writing an essay is different to writing feedback; setting an essay title is different to choosing an essay title. But all of these practices rely on each other: they are relational. The doing of an essay requires the setting of the title as much as the writing of the essay and then of the feedback. I would therefore argue that it makes sense therefore to consider doing essays as a multi-faceted but singular practice, another example of the mutual engagement – here between and amongst students and academics – through which, together, they can accomplish the work of the CoP.

The Joint Enterprise of Higher Education Communities of Practice

Establishing what a Community of Practice is about – what the joint enterprise of the CoP actually is – sounds like it ought to be a relatively straightforward process, but in fact this can be difficult to establish. Sometimes, the recognition of disciplinary boundaries can be a reliable indicator of the boundary of a CoP (discussed in depth in Chapter 6). Thus, a cohort of students all studying the same subject (a BSc in Plant Sciences or a BA in Music Production) alongside an equally identifiable cohort of staff who are teaching the programme (whether face-to-face, online or blended) can all be seen as members of the same CoP and all committed to the same joint enterprise: the doing of Plant Sciences or Music Production within a specific higher education context (that is, the institution in which we are observing the CoP at work). Not all members of either of these CoPs have to be doing the same kinds of things at the same time for the joint enterprise to be established and sustained: a degree of heterogeneity is characteristic of any CoP, after all. As previously discussed, the doing of assessed work is a point of variance between apprentices (students) and experts (academics). There will also be differences in practice amongst students within acceptable guidelines established within the CoP, for example, in relation to choosing open modules or finalising topics for third-year research or performance projects. Likewise, staff will also do things differently to varying degrees. Teaching styles, choices in resources and modes of assessment can all vary. But these variances can never be too great, otherwise the fabric of the curriculum will be affected, and the joint enterprise of the CoP may be diluted or otherwise rendered incoherent. Some resources will be irrelevant to the content of our courses or inaccessible and therefore of little use. Some assessment modes will be too unfamiliar to our students and may threaten the validity and/or reliability of the assessment process as a whole (something we shall return to in Chapter 7).

The maintenance of the joint enterprise of what we shall refer to as a *disciplinary CoP*, therefore, is tied up with the coherence of the ways in which the broader academic discipline has been codified within the curriculum. By this I mean to foreground the idea that the notion of a CoP framed within a single module or unit of study within a BA in Music Production makes sense both intuitively (mindful of the original statement by Lave and Wenger (1991) that a CoP is a largely intuitive notion) and also in terms of application of the descriptive components of CoP theory outlined by Wenger (1998) – that is to say, we can work out what the joint enterprise is, how mutual engagement is being established, what the artefacts are, and so forth. But trying to stretch the idea of the CoP across an entire academic subject area may be difficult to accomplish in some instances because the variety between the different elements of the programme may be too disparate to gather together within a single CoP and this is certainly the case in my own discipline – Education Studies – which has long been established as an interdisciplinary programme drawing on sociology, psychology, history and philosophy. Other interdisciplinary programmes such as Medieval Studies or Philosophy, Economic and Politics likewise may defy definition as disciplinary CoPs.

There are two ways of thinking about this problem. One is to consider interdisciplinary courses such as these in terms of Wenger's own ideas relating to how individual CoPs work together within arrangements that he describes as constellations (discussed in Chapter 6). Using these ideas, we can map the movement of people, materials, processes and so forth across boundaries from one CoP to another – and this would work equally well if considering the learning journey of a student on an interdisciplinary programme or on a joint honours programme. Another approach is to build on ideas posited by Boud and Middleton (2003). In their paper (which focused on vocational rather than higher education but which proposes a theoretical solution that is entirely transferable to HE), the authors posited the (to my mind extremely interesting and inexplicably under-used) notion that CoPs might be thought of as being more or less tightly framed or loosely framed (Boud & Middleton, 2003) Such a framing would refer to the coherence and clarity of the practice of the community and in turn to the nature of the joint enterprise. Both of these approaches – which need not be mutually exclusive – would be useful to consider.

The Shared Repertoire of Higher Education Communities of Practice

The shared repertoire is the last of our three (for now) core components of a CoP. The members of a CoP will have any number of different kinds of tools or objects at their disposal with which the work of the CoP will get done. Sometimes, the members of a CoP will construct new objects or adapt older ones that have been inherited from previous generations within the CoP. At other times, resources will arrive from outside the CoP and be required to be absorbed into everyday practice (as discussed in Chapter 6). These might be the actual tools found in an engineering department such as Vernier callipers, or a fume cupboard in a chemistry laboratory, or different orders of artefacts such as PDFs of book chapters for discussion in an English departmental seminar, or the module handbooks that have to be reviewed by academic quality departments. An essential aspect of learning within any CoP will involve learning how to use these different artefacts in the appropriate manner. Artefacts of different kinds or genres not only facilitate the practice of the community, but also work as cultural items, embodying – in their different ways – the histories of the CoPs in which they are used. The Vernier callipers in the engineering department remind us – simply due to their nomenclature – of the history of different engineering practices. The book chapter PDFs embody not only recent history – specifically, the technological histories that now allow us access to a range of online materials in addition to printed materials (at the university where I work, the vast majority of new library acquisitions are now electronic, not physical, resources) – but also the older histories of the study of literature and, indeed, the contexts within which the primary source materials that we are exploring were first written. Even something as simple as a module handbook – an everyday working document for anyone teaching a university module or programme – contains in part traces of the history of the curriculum to which it belongs.

CoPs draw on a wide variety of resources, therefore, but these are not restricted to the physical. CoPs also need means for organising – routines and procedures, rules of engagement and codes of conduct – that will serve to shape the working rhythms of the community. They need timetables, meetings, routines and so forth, which might in turn generate physical materials: timetables, if sufficiently complex, might need to be written down; meetings invariably – but not always – need to generate minutes, discussion papers and action logs. CoPs also need linguistic resources – ways of talking and writing that will in some ways be specific to the community in question and allow the practice of the community to be done but also to be talked and/or written about, both amongst members (for whom acquiring the specialist jargon or discourse of a community is a further aspect of learning) and also for communicating with other CoPs for whom the discourse might be unfamiliar and will therefore need to be interpreted or translated in some way.

Our rich descriptions of shared repertoires allow us to do several things. They can help us think about the ways in which how people use particular tools or objects allow us to infer things about the learning that is happening. They can also allow us to think about how people talk within a CoP and what kinds of talking – of discourse – might allow us to distinguish between experts on the one hand and newcomers on the other. And they allow us to discern differences between different CoPs and then in turn think about how they might nonetheless be joined together in some way – they help us think about boundaries. One simple way to illustrate this is through the example of the referencing conventions of different academic disciplines: one of the several moments of discombobulation in my academic writing that I experienced as I moved from being a medieval historian to being an ethnographer of education was in having to change from Chicago to APA referencing (the other big shift being encouraged to write using the first person).

Summing Up: Key Components of Any Community of Practice

A necessary first step in identifying a community of practice is to observe and describe:

- Mutual engagement – the ways in which the members of a CoP come together to get their work done – in buildings, in online meetings, sometimes daily or at other times only every now and then.
- Joint enterprise – the matters, things, interests and ruling passions that the CoP is about.
- Shared repertoire – the materials, habits, artefacts, processes and workarounds that members draw on in order to engage in practice.

Conclusion: Restoring Criticality

In this first chapter, we have discussed some of the key ingredients of any CoP: the mutual engagement, joint enterprise, and shared repertoire that can help us identify a CoP. We have also introduced some other important elements of CoP theory – legitimate peripheral participation, learning architectures, and boundaries – which will be discussed in more depth in subsequent chapters. And we have considered the different iterations of CoP theories as they have evolved over time. In relation to this, it is worth noting that in his more recent work Wenger has focussed more on the nature of professional knowledge across sets of multiple communities which he and his co-authors have described in terms of a "landscape" of practice (Wenger-Trayner et al., 2015), and on broader or looser groups which are described as "social learning spaces" (Wenger-Trayner & Wenger-Trayner, 2020). These later works are starting to garner attention but are beyond the scope of this book. Lave (2011), meantime, has continued her ethnographic inquiries into apprenticeship learning across a range of empirical contexts whilst at the same time arguing that the organisational model (although she does not use this label) "strips the concept [of CoPs] of its critical character. Many who have taken up – in order to start up – 'communities of practice' seem ignorant of the development of that concept ..." (Lave, 2019, p. 143). And to sum up, I am not suggesting that CoP theory is the answer to every problematic that we might encounter in our everyday work in universities. In Chapter 5, the strengths as well as the limitations and restrictions of CoPs will be discussed in a critical manner. Nonetheless, we can already see how a CoP perspective might not only inform our practice but also raise new questions concerning how we go about and make sense of them.

References

Amin, A., & Roberts, J. (2008). Knowing in action: Beyond communities of practice. *Research Policy*, *37*(2), 353–369.

Annala, J., & Mäkinen, M. (2016). Communities of practice in higher education: Contradictory narratives of a university-wide curriculum reform. *Studies in Higher Education*, *42*(11), 1941–1957.

Arthur, L. (2016). Communities of practice in higher education: Professional learning in an academic career. *International Journal for Academic Development*, *21*(3), 230–241.

Ashwin, P. (2009). *Analysing teaching-learning interactions in higher education: Accounting for structure and agency*. Continuum.

Boud, D., & Middleton, H. (2003). Learning from others at work: Communities of practice and informal learning. *Journal of Workplace Learning*, *15*(5), 194–202.

Cole, M., Engeström, Y., & Vasquez, O. (Eds.) (1997). *Mind, culture, and activity: Seminal papers from the laboratory of comparative human cognition*. Cambridge University Press.

Hughes, J. (2007). Lost in translation: Communities of practice – The journey from academic model to practitioner tool. In J. Hughes, N. Jewson, & L. Unwin (Eds.), *Communities of practice: Critical perspectives* (pp. 30–40). Routledge.

James, N. (2007). The learning trajectory of 'old-timers': Academic identities and communities of practice in higher education. In J. Hughes, N. Jewson, & L. Unwin (Eds.), *Communities of practice: Critical perspectives* (pp. 131–143). Routledge.

Lang, I., & Canning, R. (2010). The use of citations in educational research: The instance of The concept of 'situated learning. *Journal of Further and Higher Education*, *34*(2), 291–301.

Lave, J. (1988). *Cognition in practice: Mind, mathematics and culture in everyday life*. Cambridge University Press.

Lave, J. (2011). *Apprenticeship in critical ethnographic practice*. University of Chicago Press.

Lave, J. (2019). *Learning and everyday life: Access, participation, and changing practice*. Cambridge University Press.

Lave, J., & Wenger, E. (1991). *Situated learning: Legitimate peripheral participation*. Cambridge University Press.

Lea, M. (2005). Communities of practice' in higher education: Useful heuristic or educational model? In D. Barton, & K. Tusting (Eds.), *Beyond communities of practice: Language, power and social context* (pp. 180–197). Cambridge University Press.

Li, L., Grimshaw, J., Nielsen, C., Judd, M., Coyte, P., & Graham, I. (2009) Evolution of Wenger's concept of community of practice. *Implementation Science* 4(11), 1–8.

Mutch, A. (2003). Communities of practice and habitus: A critique. *Organisation Studies*, 24(3), 383–401.

Nunes, T., Schliemann, A., & Carraher, D. (1993). *Street mathematics and school mathematics*. Cambridge University Press.

Rogoff, B. (2003). *The cultural nature of human development*. Oxford University Press.

Rogoff, B., & Lave, J. (1984). *Everyday cognition: Its development in social context*. Harvard University Press.

Rømer, T. A. (2002). Situated learning and assessment. *Assessment and Evaluation in Higher Education*, 27(3), 233–241. https://doi.org/10.1080/02602930220138598

Thomas, G. (2007). *Education and theory: Strangers in paradigms*. McGraw Hill/Open University Press.

Tight, M. (2015). Theory application in higher education research: The case of communities of practice. *European Journal of Higher Education*, 5(2), 111–126.

Tummons, J. (2012). Theoretical trajectories within communities of practice in higher education research. *Higher Education Research and Development*, 31(3), 299–310.

Tummons, J. (2014). Learning architectures and communities of practice in higher education. In J. Huisman, & M. Tight (Eds.), *Theory and method in higher education research II* (pp. 121–139). Emerald Group Publishing Limited.

Tummons, J. (2018). *Learning architectures in higher education: Beyond communities of practice*. Bloomsbury.

Tummons, J. (2023a). *Exploring communities of practice in further and adult education: Apprenticeship, expertise and belonging*. Routledge.

Tummons, J. (2023b). Mapping academic practice: A latourian inquiry into A set of lecture slides. *Higher Education Research and Development*, 42(7), 1748–1761.

Wenger, E. (1998). *Communities of practice: Learning, meaning and identity*. Cambridge University Press.

Wenger, E. (2000). Communities of practice and social learning systems. *Organisation*, 7(2), 225–246.

Wenger, E., McDermott, R., & Snyder, W. (2002). *Cultivating communities of practice*. Harvard Business School Press.

Wenger-Trayner, E., Fenton-O'Creevy, M., Hutchinson, S., Kubiak, C., & Wenger-Trayner, B. (Eds.) (2015). *Learning in landscapes of practice: Boundaries, identity and knowledgeability in practice-based learning*. Routledge.

Wenger-Trayner, E., & Wenger-Trayner, B. (2020). *Learning to make a difference: Value creation in social learning spaces*. Cambridge University Press.

Wertsch, J., Del Río, P., & Amelia Alvarez, A. (Eds.) (1995). *Sociocultural studies of mind*. Cambridge University Press.

Chapter 2

Where Is the Learning in a Community of Practice, and How Does It Happen?

Introduction

In this chapter, we shall turn our attention to the theory of learning that lies at the heart of Communities of Practice (CoPs) theory. This theory is one of several derived from anthropology and ethnography that understand learning as being constituted through social practice. After decades of research and writing, these approaches have emerged in opposition to theories and ideas about learning derived from psychology – a focus of particular criticism from Jean Lave. As well as discussing learning within CoPs, two additional key elements of CoP theory will be introduced in this chapter: the concept of learner trajectories and the concept of change within CoPs. Through a series of worked examples, we shall frame these ideas within recognisable, authentic contexts. In this chapter, I deliberately slide between the ideas to be found in Lave and Wenger (1991), which relate more closely to the learning of apprentices or newcomers, and ideas to be found in Wenger (1998), which provide a more extensive social theory of learning.

Different Ways of Thinking About Learning

Unless you work and/or study in education studies, initial teacher education, psychology, or perhaps sociology, you would be forgiven for never having spent too much time theorising learning. Indeed, even those of us who have undertaken training and development programmes in order to obtain the closest thing that we have in universities to a teacher-training qualification – Fellowship of Advance HE (or of an earlier iteration going all the way back via the Higher Education Academy (founded in 2004) to the Institute for Learning and Teaching in Higher Education (founded in 2000)) – our acquaintance with these discussions might be cursory at best. In brief and general terms, we can argue that for much of the past century or so, the dominant ways in which people have thought about learning and hence about teaching, about ideas of intelligence or of capacity to learn, have been informed by psychology. Particular branches of psychology – behaviourism and neo-behaviourism – have waxed and waned in terms of influence and popularity. Some have held a particular influence on particular sectors of education: for example, the theory of cognitive development of the psychologist Jean Piaget continues to have an influence on schooling in England and Wales and on the National Curriculum, whilst the humanist psychology of Abraham Maslow has been highly influential in adult and community education. At the time of writing, cognitive science is enjoying a preeminent position within initial teacher education in England and Wales in no small part due to the patronage of successive government ministers. What these all have in common is a focus on the individual learner. Behaviourism and neo-behaviourism are both concerned with the study and control of observable behaviour on the part of the student. Humanist psychology foregrounds the importance of the student's self-fulfilment, and cognitive science focuses on memory and mental processes. These are, of course, all extremely brief summaries – but I do not want to spend a lot of time talking about these groups of theories because extensive descriptions are easy to find elsewhere. What I want to do instead is to consider this question: what if these psychological models are all approaching things the wrong way around, focusing on the individual's behaviour, short- or long-term memory, or cognitive processes, when we should be focusing our attention equally on the contexts – the places – where learning is happening and also on people – but people as a whole and not just their/our minds or memories or brains?

Thinking Differently About What Learning Might Be: From Psychology to Social Practice

Before Jean Lave and Etienne Wenger wrote their book *Situated Learning*, Lave spent many years doing research into how and what people learned outside formal educational settings such as universities. She spent several years during the 1970s researching apprentice tailors in Liberia (Lave & Wenger, 1991, pp. 69–73) and later focused on how people used mathematics in everyday life through the *Adult Math Project* – AMP (Lave, 1988). For the AMP, 35 people – mostly female – were observed over time as they did their supermarket shopping, put their groceries away and planned their meals, organised their household food budgets, and so forth – taking about 40 hours per person (that's 1400 hours just for the data collection, never mind the analysis and writing up – this was a substantial research project!) The idea behind the project was to look at the ways that people used different kinds of arithmetic or mathematics in their everyday lives. At the time of the AMP study – the late 1970s and early 1980s – supermarkets rarely had computerised checkout systems and the vast majority of people did not have computers at home, so budgeting, financial planning, and so forth – whether for food shopping or for other household bills – would be done using arithmetic. After collecting all of the research data, Lave then classified the *types* of arithmetic that people were using in their day-to-day lives, constructed school-style tests based on these arithmetic types, and then asked all of the AMP volunteers to take the tests in school conditions. In the tests, the AMP people were asked to do the same kinds of arithmetic that they had been observed doing in their everyday lives, but this time translated into the kinds of abstract or generic problems that are familiar to all of us from school.

What Lave found was that when people were doing their school-style tests, they could no longer do the arithmetic that they had been observed doing perfectly well on multiple occasions when doing their shopping: they were successful in their "everyday" maths but not in their "school-style" maths. Amongst the conclusions that Lave drew from this research, two stand out as being particularly important for our present conversation about learning. First, she challenged the idea that successful learning – from the point of view of psychological models – would always involve being able to *transfer* in a straightforward or unproblematic way what has been learned to a new context. That is to say, if you have learned something properly at school, you would then be able to transfer what you have learned to a different setting. Second, she challenged the idea that the failure to transfer learning in this way is a result of a cognitive inability or incapacity on the part of the individual. All of the people in the AMP study evidently did not have a cognitive incapacity, even though they scored so badly on their "school-style" tests because they could do the arithmetic in "real life".

Alongside her prior research with apprentice tailors, Lave interpreted her findings from the AMP project as showing very clearly that learning needed to be understood as being not transferable or generalisable, but instead situated within different social settings or contexts. Nor was she alone in conducting this kind of research. Numerous other writers and researchers were, at the same time, challenging the lenses offered by and insights drawn from psychology, researching contexts as diverse as psychotherapy, naval navigation, mothers helping children to learn things in the home, blacksmiths, and schoolchildren with special educational needs (Chaiklin & Lave, 1996; Rogoff & Lave, 1984). This broader field of academic work helped to generate an alternative to a psychological perspective on learning – a perspective of learning as social practice. Within this shift, sometimes described as the social turn in education and learning, Lave (1988) exemplifies the critique of the long influence of psychological models on education and training structures. First, there is the assumption that the research done by psychologists and the conclusions that they draw are straightforwardly transferable from laboratory settings to the rest of the world (as it were) and specifically to schools, colleges, and universities. Second, there is Lave's statement that psychological theories have shaped not only educational theories but also educational practices. The psychologists' focus on cognition means that intellectual work has historically been seen as being more important than practical work and, therefore, the academic curriculum is seen as being more important and consequently more prestigious than vocational or technical curricula. Relatedly, the third critique is that the academic curriculum rests on the idea that if people study a particular group of subjects, then this will form a mental discipline that will – in general – improve the minds of the students. This adds to the idea that those academic subjects are more important than others. Finally, and consequently, a contrast has been drawn between "scientific" knowledge and "everyday" knowledge. The knowledge that is said to be contained within the academic curriculum is assumed to be more important than the "everyday" knowledge found in working or family life.

The increasing diversity of forms of university provision in terms of curriculum, particularly in the United Kingdom following the government reforms of the early 1990s but also in other national higher education structures as well, throws this discussion of curriculum theory into sharp relief. The expansion of vocational and technical curricula within universities – and also professional curricula as well – has served to challenge stereotypical notions of the "academic" nature of university work in ways that we can argue make a more generous understanding of learning – such as that offered by a social model – particularly apposite.

From Social Practice to Community of Practice: Social Models of Learning

Communities of Practice theory is just one example of a family of social practice theories in just the same way that there are different schools of psychological theory. Indeed, the wider individual work of Lave and Wenger both before and after the publication of their 1991 book constitutes a broad collection of theoretical perspectives in and of itself. Different theorists and writers have emphasised rather different things, but social practice theories of learning do all share some common ground. Instead of focusing entirely on the mind, on mental function and behaviour, social practice theories focus on the whole person. What a student or apprentice can do is as important as what they can remember. Accordingly, from such a standpoint, knowing something, or knowledgeability, is not purely or solely a mental process, but a process that has an impact on the whole person – how they think, talk, act, use tools and materials, and interact with their environment. Social practice theories do not try to split up the academic and the vocational, or the cognitive and the practical: taxonomies such as cognitive/psychomotor/affective domains of learning are rejected because these are seen as false, even misleading divisions. Similarly, social practice theories do not make a distinction between formal learning and informal learning – learning is "the same" wherever it is taking place. It is never an individual process but always a shared one – a social one. Learning happens at all sorts of times and in all sorts of places, even if we don't always realise it, and – most importantly – it always happens as a consequence of practice. A social practice model of learning is about more than just apprenticeship or learning by doing however. It also includes learning by talking and thinking, learning by writing, and learning by listening. Learning involves the whole person and the whole body. Put simply, people learn things from being able to take part in practice, to try things out. Being able to ask other more experienced people how things are done, which tool or procedure would be best used for a particular task and when, and so forth is an important part of this practice. And in a university, those more experienced people – the experts of the CoP in question – are usually the academics but also might include post-doctoral researchers, PhD students, and so forth. However – and here we see an important contribution of CoP theory at work – whilst academics and students quite clearly occupy different positions within their department as a consequence of their respective levels of expertise and experience and so forth in respect of the discipline – the joint enterprise – of the CoP, they are both nonetheless also learners. By this I mean to foreground the simple fact of learning as always being constituted through practice and, therefore, integral to the participation within the CoP of all members, irrespective of their statuses as either old-timers or newcomers. As researchers exploring higher education from a CoP perspective, therefore, our assumption will be that learning is always happening within any CoP, shared – heterogeneously – between all community members. We are always learning.

Communities of Practice theory rests on a particular iteration of social learning theory, explored in depth by Wenger (1998) but first introduced, as a particular way of discussing apprenticeship learning, in Lave and Wenger's (1991) original book. In fact, as I noted in Chapter 1, the idea of the CoP was only briefly discussed in the first book, whereas their model of learning was more extensively explored. For Lave and Wenger, apprenticeship is the main focus for attention and their model – Legitimate Peripheral Participation (LPP) – does in fact neatly sum up what the theory is all about and how it slots into the CoP model, and so it is worth our while to unpack LPP. An understanding of LPP is one of the central ideas for making sense of how CoPs work.

Exploring Legitimate Peripheral Participation

Before we go any further, therefore, we need to spend some time thinking about what LPP actually is. There are two elements to this conversation: the first is to approach LPP as one element of a social theory of learning (Wenger, 1998), and the second is to weave LPP into a CoP. As our discussion of LPP proceeds, we will introduce a small number of additional elements of CoP theory to add to those introduced in the preceding chapter.

What is LPP? The most straightforward way to define it is to go backwards and start with participation, which we have already introduced. Every member of a CoP engages with – and participates in – whatever it is that the CoP is about. And as we know, learning is an epistemological consequence of participation. Participation is a fundamental component of CoP membership: it is not possible to be a member of a CoP without also participating in what the CoP does. For the student or newcomer, participation is self-evidently qualitatively different to that of the academic or old-timer: the participation of the student is therefore characterised as being more marginal or peripheral. At the same time, because the participation – and hence the learning – of the student is taking place within a CoP, it follows axiomatically that what the student is practising and thereby learning must be an authentic aspect of the work of the CoP – the joint enterprise – more broadly, it has to be legitimate.

LPP, then, is the theory of apprenticeship learning established by Lave and Wenger (1991) but which need not be restricted to the exploration of apprenticeships as a (long-standing) form of workplace or work-related learning (although medieval guilds do pop up more than once as historical examples of CoPs (Wenger, 2000)). Rather, we adopt apprenticeship as a more broadly metaphorical – and indeed metaphysical – concept in order to make sense of the ways in which newcomers – students – learn within their CoPs. And remembering one of the important messages from Chapter 1 – that CoPs are already out there in the world and that it is simply the case that we have to go looking for them – it is a relatively straightforward exercise to imagine LPP at work. This might be in ways that speak directly to the disciplinary area being studied or more broadly to the practices involved in being a student in a more general sense. So we might see the former at work in a seminar when a group of students on a history course is introduced for the first time to the analysis of primary sources – the historical records and archives and so forth that underpin the practices of the historian. By contrast, the latter might be seen in those instances when our history students are writing dissertations, the long-form capstone projects that are typical of many other curricula (although we will always of course be able to tell the difference between disciplines on close inspection).

These are just two examples of the joint enterprise of CoPs, requiring people to learn about all kinds of things. These involve both "theoretical" and "practical" knowledge and know-how, which are always overlapping and interdependent. Knowing how to read a medieval manuscript requires not only ways to understand the meaning and import of the words that are written and the ideas or issues expressed in them – a process of semiosis – but also the knowledge of how to read medieval handwriting – palaeography – and also the knowledge of how to access online manuscripts, or manipulate and care for physical manuscripts. As advocates of CoP theory, we would reject a divide between "theoretical" knowledge and "practical" knowledge. For Lave (1988), in particular, this erroneous bifurcation is nothing more than a reflection of the legacy of particular iterations of positivist psychology on discussions of learning and pedagogy during the twentieth century that privileged the theoretical and the conceptual. There is a separate discussion to be had about historical as well as contemporary social and cultural attitudes towards different types of knowledgeability which are linked to employment patterns, social class, the formation of "the professions", and many other factors which are beyond the scope of this book. From the perspective of situated learning and CoPs, we would instead argue that all of these ways of knowing are "the same" because they are all necessary in order to engage in practice – or, to put it another way, they are all necessary for mutual engagement.

Practice through mutual engagement both rests on and requires learning about and using tools and materials, concepts and processes. Some of these will be familiar because they can also be found in many other CoPs both within universities and elsewhere. This might be because the work of the CoP in question is closely aligned with the work of another: it does not require much of a leap of imagination to see how the laboratory within a CoP in a chemistry department would be familiar in terms of equipment, sounds, materials, printed resources, aromas, and so forth to a CoP centred around an industrial laboratory. These two CoPs are distinct but share a great deal. And whilst someone unfamiliar with the sciences might at first glance mistake a chemistry laboratory for a biology laboratory, a more careful inquiry would soon allow us to resolve this error notwithstanding the fact that our biology CoP would nonetheless share much – although perhaps not too much – with our chemistry CoP. The medieval manuscripts CoP would likewise require some careful attention so that it can be correctly identified (a CoP for a BA in History? An MA in English? An MPhil in Palaeography and Manuscript Studies?), and again we can imagine how materials, ideas, and resources might be shared across these to different degrees. But in both instances, the learning that is taking place is quite specific to that CoP – it is situated within the specific community, even though the shared repertoires of these two communities display many points of convergence and overlap with others.

It is in the step-by-step embodiment, demonstration, and articulation of knowing within the CoP that we can discern learning through LPP as the newcomers – the students – become more expert. Over time we listen to our students discuss matters at hand with greater ease, fluency, and insight, utilising an ever-wider range of resources and materials, drawing on more complex ideas, and generating more robust analyses and conclusions, all enfolded and captured (or, better, *reified*) within essays, reports, posters, and so forth. Taken together, these can subsequently make up an array of different formative and summative assessment tasks (as discussed in Chapter 7) which are easily recognisable within any university as ways in which we can see, record, and generate evidence for our students' learning. But from a CoP perspective, our understanding of learning equally includes the embodied knowledgeability that we might see in how a student uses laboratory equipment or handles a manuscript as much as how knowledgeability is presented through spoken contributions to seminars or written work handed in at the end of the module or programme of study. All of these forms of mutual engagement rest on the students' growing familiarity with and understanding of the shared repertoire of the CoP.

Simply put, therefore, the shared repertoire consists of all of those objects, materials, tools, ways of talking, patterns of action, routines, and so forth that all of the members of the CoP need to employ in order to be able to participate in the authentic practices of the community: the journal articles, posters, lab equipment and materials, the specialist discourses, and terminologies of a community. As the student (the apprentice) becomes more fluent and adept in all of the aspects of the CoP – how they write, how they speak, how they move, how they do the things that the community is about – they, therefore, move from being a peripheral member to being a fuller member.

Learning and Membership: From Being Peripheral to Being Full

Membership of any CoP always entails learning, for both the newcomer and the old-timer, the novice and the expert. For the newcomers, the direction of travel that they take once they are within the CoP is pretty straightforward: they arrive knowing not very much about the practice of the community, and as they travel through the CoP and engage in the work being done, they learn more. Learning happens all the time, even if they don't realise that it's taking place. The more authentic or legitimate their participation, the more efficacious their learning is: it is more closely aligned to the joint enterprise of the CoP, more authentic and consequently more meaningful. As the newcomers participate in practice, the more knowing/knowledgeable they become and, at the same time, the fuller their membership becomes. The newcomers start their learning journeys at the periphery, and travel in a fuller direction as they learn, becoming more expert, more proficient, more knowledgeable, and competent as they go. This direction of travel through and across a CoP is referred to as the learner's trajectory (Lave & Wenger, 1991, pp. 18–19; Wenger, 1998, pp. 153–156), and we can see these working in several ways. For example, it is easy to imagine the trajectory of an individual student who travels from BSc to MSc to PhD and then to a post-doctoral position in their field of study as a clear journey from apprentice to expert, from the edges of the disciplinary CoP to the centre ground. For the student who follows a similar route but across different institutions, a slightly more complex journey needs to be mapped out and we need to consider how being at one university – in one CoP – for their BSc and MSc then facilitates entry into a separate CoP – at another university – that is nonetheless closely related to the first one in terms of field of study. Meanwhile, our third student has decided that after completing their BSc, a different career will be best and has enrolled on a Postgraduate Certificate in Education (PGCE) in a different department at the same university, or perhaps in a different department at a different university: for this student, the membership of their initial CoP has allowed them access to their second CoP (BSc to PGCE), but the process of crossing over to this new CoP is qualitatively different than the crossing made by the first two students who have stayed within the same academic fields. For example, a fourth student decides, after completing their BSc, to embark on a career in scientific publishing, and a fifth decides on a career in stand-up comedy.

As we can easily imagine, different members of a CoP do not therefore necessarily share the same trajectories. Different trajectories such as these help us start to think about how members might travel from one CoP to another, so long as it is not too distant or different, or even how they can juggle being members of several overlapping communities at once. We shall think about multimembership in more depth in Chapter 6: for now, it is sufficient to recognise that being a member of lots of CoPs over time is not uncommon and that some of these CoPs will be closely linked or overlapping whilst others might be quite distinct. Any CoP always contains members who are travelling along different trajectories.

Lave and Wenger (1991) originally (and arguably not entirely helpfully) conceived of trajectories as being "extremely diverse and [not] predictable" (p. 19) but otherwise (as with the CoP model itself) provided relatively little detail. Wenger (1998, pp. 154–155) identified five specific kinds of trajectory, and as CoP research and theory has evolved, other writers have proposed additional theoretical components to help us make sense of trajectories (Handley et al., 2006; Tummons, 2018). For now, it is to Wenger's (1998) framework that we shall turn.

Trajectories Within and Across Communities of Practice

We can describe the different trajectories that members of any CoP follow in several ways, therefore, from the moment at which the newcomer has met any conditions that might pertain to crossing the CoP boundary and therefore having been permitted to join.

The archetypal trajectory that describes the "traditional" journey from apprenticeship to mastery is the *inbound* trajectory. Inbound trajectories are those trajectories that, all other things being equal, afford CoP members the opportunity to access fuller levels of participation. The apprentice/student will start at the periphery and is then committed and/or allowed and/or expected to continue learning in order to move to a position that is increasingly full (but never completely so), with a greater depth of mutual engagement, a more fluent use of the shared repertoire, and a more profound understanding and commitment to the joint enterprise of the CoP.

The idea of the *insider* trajectory helps us to think about what happens to a CoP member once they have reached this fuller state of membership. We can never say that membership is full in the sense that a complete or absolute fullness of participation has been accomplished. This is because, as we shall see, the practices of CoPs can change over time: they are by definition dynamic, never still, so there is always more to learn. Rather, being in a position of fuller or more central membership means that a sufficient level of expertise has been reached so that the member is able to contribute to the evolution of the practice of the community: to change and to innovate, in turn necessitating more learning for the CoP as a whole.

However, not everyone aspires to such profound engagement with the work of the community. And not everyone is permitted or capable to do so. *Peripheral* trajectories are those trajectories that are never – by design – intended to lead to fuller participation. This might be due to the way in which a CoP has evolved over time, or this might be due to the individual member deciding that they do not want to aim for full participation. Instead, they are happier – or required – to remain at the edges.

Other members of the community may choose to maintain a less-than-full trajectory for other reasons related to the boundaries of the CoP in question. All CoPs have a boundary, and to varying degrees, these need to be maintained so that traffic between CoPs can be facilitated and entry and exit to the CoP can be regulated (we shall explore this in Chapter 6). *Boundary* trajectories, therefore, are those pathways followed by members who – for various reasons – either prefer or are required to practice at the boundary of a CoP.

Finally, there are the *outbound* trajectories. These describe the routes followed by members as they move out of a CoP. Once again, there can be several reasons for this. It might be the case that membership was only ever intended to be temporary; alternatively, it might be the case that the member in question has decided, or has been required, to move on to something different and has had their originally anticipated trajectory disrupted. Or it may be the case that over time a CoP has undergone such a profound change that a member may no longer want to be part of it – or may no longer be wanted.

Thinking about participation in terms of these different trajectories allows us to make sense of the kinds of journeys taken by people that are recognisable to anyone who has worked in a university. It doesn't matter if we are focusing on students/apprentices/newbies or on lecturers/old-timers/experts. They/we are all CoP members and therefore all learning as a consequence of their/our participation in practice. For the apprentices, learning is through LPP, affording them entry into the community. For the experts, full participation continues to generate opportunities for learning and also for innovation in learning and hence in practice. If the CoP is in a state of change, expert status can be diminished – practices change, new methods emerge, and fresh concepts are discussed – thereby requiring more learning in turn. In this way, we can see why learning is always happening, as a consequence and corollary of practice, sometimes at a rapid pace and sometimes only slowly, sometimes in an iterative and organic manner, and at other times with more drastic leaps in terms of the knowledgeability that resides within the CoP.

Summing Up: Learning, and Learning Journeys

- Within a CoP, learning is understood as a social practice – a way of theorising learning derived from anthropologies and ethnographies of education.
- LPP describes the learning of newcomers/apprentices.
- Within any CoP, learners might follow different trajectories of learning: these can change over time.

Thinking Ahead: Multimembership

In Chapter 1, we discussed three paradigmatic elements of any CoP – mutual engagement, joint enterprise, and shared repertoire – and in addition to describing what these actually are, we noted that it is through their identification or recognition that we can begin to discern a CoP at work. Because the boundaries of a CoP are rarely only physical, it is also in how the distinctiveness of a CoP becomes manifest in relation to an adjacent CoP – the different ways in which stuff gets done, spoken about, embodied, and so forth – that we can distinguish between them. The same holds for the trajectories of a CoP: once we can identify or map out trajectories of learning, we can use those trajectories to help us identify the boundaries of the CoP within which they are situated. This is not to say that we can only ever identify a CoP from the ground up – that is, from assembling the core components – as we might easily on occasion be able to identify physical and/or institutional boundaries. What I mean to stress here is that it is perfectly feasible to begin to account for student learning from a CoP perspective by beginning with the trajectories and then scaling up to look for the CoP as a whole, and this is additionally important if the trajectories that we are tracing lead us to identify more than one CoP and therefore conclude that participation and therefore learning necessarily relies on being part of more than one CoP at the same time, referred to within CoP theory as *multimembership* (Wenger, 1998). And as we shall see in Chapter 6 in particular, discussions about multimembership are, in a manner akin to discussions about the interplays between different CoPs and the crossings that occur across their boundaries, unavoidable and provide a clear illustration of the simple fact that no CoP exists in isolation. For the present, it is sufficient to note that any consideration of learning trajectories will touch upon these issues as well.

Trajectories for Learning in Communities of Practice in Higher Education

Using those elements of CoP theory that we now have in place, we can start to think about the ways in which they relate to each other and allow us to make sense of and generate useful descriptions of the everyday (though far from mundane) learning, teaching, and assessment practices of higher education.

Imagine that we are following the learning journey of a new student who is seeking to establish a career as a youth and community worker. There are several different qualifications available to choose from which of course map directly onto the specific occupational role and/or status that is aspired towards, and a range of certificates and diplomas are available at level three (equivalent to A level) which would be available to study at a local further education college and which would be suitable entry qualifications for a career as a youth support worker. Our student, however, hopes to become a *professional youth worker* and so, as we might imagine, requires a university-level qualification in order to obtain the requisite professional status. The provision of specific programmes of study that map onto specific regulated professions is a well-established feature of the higher education sector more generally and is referred to as the professional curriculum, encompassing subject areas such as nursing and law as well as youth work (Bourner et al., 2000; Eraut, 1994; Lester, 2009; Taylor, 1997) – not to be confused with the terms professional learning and professional development which are invariably used to describe academics' ongoing learning as teachers, researchers, and/or leaders in the sector (Daniels, 2017; Knight et al., 2006).

Our student can choose from a variety of undergraduate and postgraduate routes, and even a cursory search online shows that relevant degrees are offered at a number of institutions in broadly similar patterns, both BA and occasionally BSc programmes, and also MA programmes (sometimes with a Postgraduate Diploma option). By "broadly similar" I mean to refer to the fact that there are several elements of the curricula being offered across institutions that have features in common, such as theory modules exploring constructs such as social work and social justice, placements accompanied by reflective practice assignments, research methods modules tailored to the kinds of methodologies that would be appropriate to employ within youth work contexts, mentoring and counselling, leadership and management, and safeguarding. Many undergraduate programmes will include an empirical research project, as do MA programmes (although these also offer a Diploma exit award for people who don't wish to do a capstone research project). At a practical level, there are often part-time as well as full-time options available. Youth studies or youth work self-evidently constitutes a distinct field of higher education practice, and a successful journey through this field in turn will allow our students to enter the profession. And since it is a field of higher education practice, we find a concomitant body of scholarly work – monographs, research reports, academic journals, handbooks, and the like (and we return to the specific practices of research in Chapter 8).

For our student, the journey from newly arrived undergraduate to work-ready graduate will require the successful completion of a number of different learning trajectories, and exactly how we trace these will depend on how we interpret and apply CoP theory more broadly (we shall see examples of these different approaches at work in Chapter 3). To begin: how should we define the first Youth Work Degree CoP that our student will cross into? We might be satisfied that the entire degree programme, as a particular kind of manifestation or formation of the academic field, constitutes a single CoP. Or we might instead propose that the degree programme is formed from a constellation of CoPs, one for each module, that overlap and work together to accomplish the degree as a whole. Our second problem is where to put the academic staff who teach on the degree, mark the essays, attend the moderation meetings, and so forth. They are self-evidently part of the Youth Work Degree CoP, but how exactly do we make sense of this?

If we decide that the practices of the staff are distinct from those of the students – staff set the assignments, students write them, staff write the lectures, students listen to them, and so forth – then we need to locate them in two co-existent CoPs, one for staff and one for students, and then describe how they might overlap in order to work together. However, if we decide that these practices are intertwined and incapable of being explored in a discrete manner then we will keep staff and students in the same CoP and make sense of their different practices as being relational – the doing of essays involves both staff and students, as do lectures and presentations and so forth – and therefore all contained within the same CoP. These different approaches are extant in the literature and – depending on your point of view – indicate either that CoP theory is too permissive and therefore lacks explanatory potential, or that CoP theory is sufficiently elastic to allow for a range of diverse applications, albeit with limits (Tight, 2015, 2018). And although I subscribe to the latter perspective, and as such position staff and students within the same CoPs (Tummons, 2012, 2014, 2018), I have read any number of papers that draw on the former perspective and from which I have gained useful insights.

Whether across one CoP or several, our student will follow an inbound trajectory (or perhaps a series of these, one for each module, for example), and this is because the goal is to reach a level of participation within the Youth Work Degree CoP that is sufficiently full to allow our student to gain the degree certificate that serves as a documentary artefact to allow entry into the youth work profession. At the same time, this trajectory will be peripheral because it is by design limited in terms of both duration and depth of participation. The limitation in duration simply reflects the time that our student will spend on the course. The limitation in depth of participation reflects the fact that our student needs to participate – to learn – only so much as is required for the successful negotiation of the trajectory. Once a degree certificate has been obtained, our student will leave the higher education CoP (a rapid outbound trajectory) and enter the profession, once again as a newcomer – an apprentice – but now in a new CoP that pertains to the profession itself, framed in terms of the place of work and the employer (and therefore beyond the scope of our present inquiry). This might be an entirely new workplace CoP but will not be entirely unfamiliar: the programme of study will have helped our student prepare for employment, and workplace placement will have provided early exposure to other workplace CoPs – perhaps even the same one where full employment is eventually obtained – on a visiting basis. It is in the overlaps between these CoPs that the practices of knowing shared between them can be found.

If, on the other hand, our student decided during the programme that a future as a postgraduate researcher and perhaps as an academic in Youth Work was more preferable, then the inbound trajectory would be maintained for longer – across a PhD and then into an early career researcher/academic position. At this point, our former student and now new academic would begin to follow an insider trajectory if a career as a researcher and teacher is to be pursued. The learning that is characteristic of the insider trajectory is no longer that of the apprentice but of the expert who seeks to build on, to augment, or even to challenge or disrupt the practices of the community through their research practice (discussed in Chapter 8). Change is a characteristic of every CoP, whether or not the pace of change is so slow as to be barely noticeable or so fast that we can hardly keep up. Change can be gradual or incremental, or can come in fits and starts. It can be caused by inventions and improvisations, by happy accidents, or in response to difficulties. If practice changes, it follows that participation has to change. For members of a CoP who follow a *peripheral* trajectory, the changes may well not even be noticeable because their time spent within the CoP might not be long enough for these changes to make themselves felt. For those on *inbound* and *insider* trajectories, these changes will require new learning.

There is no fixed pattern or format to the trajectories that we might find within a CoP. The trajectories that we might follow are not pre-ordained or fixed; rather, a CoP constitutes a "field of possible trajectories" (Wenger, 1998, p. 156). And if we find ourselves uncertain as to which kind of trajectory we might be tracing at any one moment, then we can allow ourselves to move creatively within the framework established by CoP theory. Perhaps a trajectory can be both inbound and also peripheral at the same time? If a trajectory is always going to be temporary, then at what point does the outbound trajectory take over? By posing questions such as these, we can avoid a prescriptive or deterministic use of the theoretical tools at our disposal and use them instead to generate insights into the learning and teaching cultures that we are interested in and perhaps contribute to CoP theory in turn. For example, the jump from university CoP to workplace CoP taken by our student in the above example neatly illustrates a key concept within CoP theory that was originally proposed not by Jean Lave or Etienne Wenger, but by Jay Lemke. Lemke, originally a physicist before becoming interested in science education more broadly, was an early commentator on Lave and Wenger's original work. One of the problems that he identified with CoP theory was: what if mastery of the practice in one community depended on having first gained a level of mastery in a different one? What happens within a community when there is no expectation of full participation for some members? His solution, simple and elegant, was to propose that sometimes membership of one CoP would only be available to people who had been members of another CoP first (Lemke, 1997).

Summing Up: Describing Communities of Practice

- CoP theory is sufficiently elastic to allow for a diversity of applications – for example, in establishing whether or not students and staff are or are not members of the same disciplinary CoPs.
- The warrant of any CoP account rests in the depth and criticality of theoretical and empirical engagement.
- Several authors have proposed extensions to CoP theory and these can help us resolve some of those matters that are not sufficiently explained by Lave and Wenger, or Wenger. We shall return to some of these in Chapter 5.

Back to Mutual Engagement, Joint Enterprise, and Especially Shared Repertoire

We can now return to the three paradigmatic components of any CoP that we discussed in Chapter 1. Having established our theory of learning and the trajectories that our different learning journeys trace, we can now start to think about how our understanding of these three CoP elements helps us further in thinking about learning as a social (and not solely "cognitive") practice. For example, we might see how our student, in becoming more expert, begins to enjoy a more profound mutual engagement within the CoP, with the time served in the CoP affording more extensive entanglements in the social relationships of the community, and at greater levels of complexity. Perhaps it will be in the joint enterprise of the community that we see the traces of greater expertise gained through participation, as our student engages more profoundly with the purpose or function of the community, contributing to the work being done through student politics and representation, or student ambassadorship. But it is in the understanding and utilisation of the shared repertoire of the CoP that we can most straightforwardly see and/or infer the growing expertise of our student, as learning both requires greater utilisation of the shared repertoire of the CoP and also contribution to it.

All three of these elements are equally important, but I am going to suggest that the shared repertoire is the most useful of the three for helping us make sense of the practices of higher education. This is, quite simply, because it is in thinking about the stuff of any CoP – the artefacts, the tools, the materials, the ways of talking and writing, the concepts and theories – that we can see the engagement of all of the members of the CoP in the most straightforward manner. Our students become more adept in using the tools of the community, whether these are physical tools such as those found in an archaeology lab or a physics lab or conceptual tools in a mathematics seminar or philosophy tutorial. It is how our students act, talk, and write in the broadest sense – that is, across different formats or modalities of assessment, in different kinds of teaching environments, and so forth – that we can infer that learning has taken place. As our students learn, they inhabit the discourses of the community more deeply, use the tools of the community more fluently, and draw on the concepts and stories of the community more extensively – and all of these become less effortful in turn. These are not uniform processes of course: students/apprentices follow similar but not identical trajectories and as such no two will ever learn the same stuff in the same way or to the same extent. But so long as their learning is sufficient for the trajectory that they have chosen and is sufficient to meet the expectations of the community in terms of depth of mutual engagement and adherence to the joint enterprise, then the CoP will continue to thrive and grow.

Conclusion: Describing Learning

In this chapter, we have explored the concept of LPP – the way in which we explain how learning is made available to any newcomer to a CoP. We have explored the trajectories of CoP members in depth, and begun to think about how CoPs change over time, which makes every member a learner of some kind and which illustrates the social theory of learning that is integral to CoP theory. In the following chapter, we shall look at a number of different research articles, books, and book chapters, and see what they can tell us about the higher education sector more broadly from a CoP perspective. For now, the key message is to remember the centrality of learning within any community: without learning, there cannot be a CoP. Learning always involves others. And it always involves learning whatever needs to be learned, whether or not it is "theoretical" or "practical" – distinctions that CoP theory rejects because the idea of dividing things between the theoretical and the practical was mistaken in the first place. So-called "academic" subjects are not "harder" or "more challenging" than so-called "vocational" subjects: the only reason why people thought that (and why some still do) is because psychological research placed an emphasis on cognition "in the mind" at the expense of everything else that makes a person who they are. The social theory of learning that CoPs rest on is not just about what can be stored in long-term memory or what mental schema can be constructed. It is about the whole person: who we are, what we do, how we speak and act, how we stand and move, how we hold tools, express ideas, link concepts, solve problems, and help each other along. Anybody who has worked in a university knows that there is more to learning than passing exams (for courses that still have them) or completing projects (although, as we shall see in Chapter 7, these are both still important). It is in the way our students learn to speak and move, the kinds of questions that they ask, the novel solutions that they employ, and the increasing fluency and ease with which they more confidently go about their work, that we can observe, hear, and infer that learning has been happening.

References

Bourner, T., Katz, T., & Watson, D. (Eds.). (2000). *New directions in professional higher education*. Open University Press/Society for Research into Higher Education.

Chaiklin, S., & Lave, J. (Eds.). (1996). *Understanding practice: Perspectives on activity and context*. Cambridge University Press.

Daniels, J. (2017). Professional learning in higher education: Making good practice relevant. *International Journal for Academic Development, 22*(2), 170–181.

Eraut, M. (1994). *Developing professional knowledge and competence*. RoutledgeFalmer.

Handley, K., Sturdy, A., Fincham, R., & Clark, T. (2006). Within and beyond communities of practice: Making sense of learning through participation, identity and practice. *Journal of Management Studies, 43*(3), 641–653.

Knight, P., Tait, J., & Yorke, M. (2006). The professional learning of teachers in higher education. *Studies in Higher Education, 31*(3), 319–339.

Lave, J. (1988). *Cognition in practice: Mind, mathematics and culture in everyday life*. Cambridge University Press.

Lave, J., & Wenger, E. (1991). *Situated learning: Legitimate peripheral participation*. Cambridge University Press.

Lemke, J. (1997). Cognition, context and learning: A social semiotic perspective. In D. Kirshner, & J. Whitson (Eds.), *Situated cognition: Social, semiotic and psychological perspectives* (pp. 37–56). Lawrence Erlbaum Associates.

Lester, S. (2009). Routes to qualified status: Practices and trends among UK professional bodies. *Studies in Higher Education, 34*(2), 223–236.

Rogoff, B., & Lave, J. (1984). *Everyday cognition: Its development in social context*. Harvard University Press.

Taylor, I. (1997). *Developing learning in professional education*. Open University Press/Society for Research into Higher Education.

Tight, M. (2015). Theory application in higher education research: The case of communities of practice. *European Journal of Higher Education, 5*(2), 111–126.

Tight, M. (2018). *Higher education research: The developing field*. Bloomsbury.

Tummons, J. (2012). Theoretical trajectories within communities of practice in higher education research. *Higher Education Research and Development, 31*(3), 299–310.

Tummons, J. (2014). Learning architectures and communities of practice in higher education. In J. Huisman, & M. Tight (Eds.), *Theory and method in higher education research II* (pp. 121–139). Emerald Group Publishing Limited.

Tummons, J. (2018). *Learning architectures in higher education: Beyond communities of practice*. Bloomsbury.

Wenger, E. (1998). *Communities of practice: Learning, meaning and identity*. Cambridge University Press.

Wenger, E. (2000). Communities of practice and social learning systems. *Organization 7*(2), 225–246.

Chapter 3

Communities of Practice in Higher Education

What Can We Learn from the Research?

Introduction

In this chapter, I am going to discuss some of the work done on Communities of Practice (CoPs) in higher education by other researchers and writers. I am not conducting a wide-ranging, systematic review of the literature, nor am I setting out to list and then dismantle CoP-based papers written by others that I consider to be insufficiently thorough in their use of theory and/or empirical data, or based on an application of CoP theory that differs sharply from my own. Rather, as throughout this book as a whole, I want to focus on what can be done with CoP theory when it is used well. So the aim of this chapter is to look at a few examples of CoP work that are rooted within higher education and that primarily focus on learning and teaching in a broad sense but not on assessment which, as we shall learn, takes some time to unpack and will be explored later in the book. Through this conversation, we can start to look at some of the ways in which CoP theory can inform our research into, and our discussions about, different aspects of practice in higher education.

Putting Theory to Work

Up to now, I have established that if we are going to think about higher education from a Communities of Practice standpoint, then we need to do several things. First of all, we need to say what the practice is and where the community is. After that, we need to drill down into the CoP and provide an account of the mutual engagement, joint enterprise, and shared repertoire that characterise and define the community. We need to be able to discuss the things that make the CoP what it is. If we do this, then we will end up with accounts that are sufficiently rigorous in their use of the theory so as to be convincing, and that will allow us to activate the explanatory and/or predictive capacities of the theory. For example, we know that learners within a CoP can follow several different trajectories. So if we are satisfied that we are looking at a CoP, then it must be the case that these trajectories are, according to the context, all present as well.

DOI: 10.4324/9781003412106-3

Unlike Lave and Wenger, we do not necessarily have to commit to an empirical inquiry in order to conduct our inquiries. For starters, many of us will not always have sufficient time to conduct the kind of rich, ethnographic work that (I suggest) is best aligned to CoP theory and which is therefore best placed (again, to my mind) to provide a robust empirical warrant for our discussions. Instead, reading research papers written by others may be a more realistic and achievable task in the time available. A CoP-informed perspective can, for the purposes of our discussion, be derived from familiarising ourselves with relevant literature rather than conducting research first-hand.

Before we can start to put CoP theory to work through establishing what it can tell us about higher education learning and teaching practices, we need to remember that the very notion of the CoP is not entirely stable. In their book, Lave and Wenger (1991, p. 42) described a CoP as a "largely intuitive notion", and as we saw in Chapter 1, it was not until Wenger's (1998) later work was published that a more detailed and applicable framework emerged. Subsequently, Lave and Wenger have travelled along quite separate paths, and it is fascinating to see how the two creators of the CoP model have left it behind in certain respects (Barton & Tusting, 2005), although it does make things rather difficult for those of us who still use it. Should we (to put things simply) use the academic version from Wenger (1998) or the practitioner version from Wenger et al. (2002)? And on what basis should we draw on the theoretical as distinct from empirical contributions made by others?

There may well not be any *a priori* reason why you cannot draw from both versions. Although I have yet to establish a good reason within my own empirical research for using the practitioner instead of the academic model, there are self-evidently sound academic reasons for doing so, not least as a willingness to engage in some theoretical pluralism affords us access to a wider body of literature. Thus, as we shall see below, we can equally learn from research informed by the practitioner version as by the academic version as part of our discerning appreciation of the literature. Reading around the subject is a course of action that needs to be carried out both carefully and critically, and how it gets done will depend on the job that we have set out to do. All of this is a roundabout way of saying that in what follows, I have not conducted a systematic review, nor do I claim to be making any claims or proposing any lines of argument based on an exhaustive exploration of the extant literature on higher education that draws on CoPs. At a practical level, the corpus of literature is now sufficiently extensive so as to require a considerable amount of time for such a project (Tight, 2015).

Nor do I intend to critique papers that do not, to my reading, talk about CoPs with sufficient care for properly defining or explicating them, offering only a cursory use of theory (Thomas, 2007). I have done so elsewhere and do not propose to repeat the exercise here (Tummons, 2018). It is, however, a problem that we need to be aware of because it leads to a lack of theoretical precision, blunting the tools contained within the CoP toolbox.

An author might claim that they are telling us about a particular aspect of CoPs or about a constellation of CoPs, but without seriously engaging with the literature, their use of specialist concepts and terms is unhelpful and lacks rigour. And just because a chapter or article contains references to Wenger's work, it doesn't mean that the author has put that work to good use: plentiful citations do not always equate to robust reading (see Lang & Canning, 2010, for a particularly appropriate example). Indeed, I have recently come across one paper in a peer-reviewed journal that purports to be about CoPs but does not include any work by either Lave and/or Wenger in the list of references: clearly, not all editors and peer reviewers share my standpoint.

For this discussion, therefore, I limit myself to addressing one main concern, which is to consider a small number of carefully curated examples of literature that provide a *proof of concept* for CoPs – articles or chapters that show the CoP framework being put to good use in different ways, in order to explore educational and training contexts that are aligned to the focus of this book: the higher education sector.

Academic Departments and Academic Disciplines as Communities of Practice

University departments tend to be distinct in appearance, in feel, and in sound in all kinds of ways. Some of this is due to architecture: the buildings, the spaces between them, the laboratories, seminar rooms, offices, and common rooms. Some of this is due to what the people who move within these spaces actually do, how they work and talk, and perhaps even how they dress. All sorts of everyday actions – conversations between colleagues in corridors, staff and students sharing some informal words on the way to or from a class, students talking to each other about their next assignment – tell us something about the CoP that is around us. And some of this is due to the material stuff – the artefacts – that are to be found in these places: the sign-up sheets pinned to office doors for booking tutorials, the posters made by PhD students for conferences that have since been put on display along the corridors, the display cabinet containing books written by members of staff, and the leaflets for IT services or Academic Skills Support sessions. The department in which I work moved to a new building and one thing that was conspicuously lacking for the first several months was any material sign that I was in fact inside a school of education, apart from the signage at the front of the building. Once inside, the corridors were pretty much bare, and the ubiquitous monitors that were mounted on the walls in different parts of the building showed generic university notices as often as they displayed notices specific to the school. Only recently have posters, notices, and so forth started to appear, stamping a sense of identity onto an otherwise featureless building. Meanwhile, the rooms and corridors of the Department of Anthropology, only a few minutes walk away, are so richly decorated that it is almost impossible to mistake it for being anything other than an anthropology department.

One way – but not the only way – of identifying a CoP is in the material fabric and culture that we can see. Stuff such as this captures and makes concrete, or reifies, the histories, practices, and ways of knowing of the department – they are part of the shared repertoire that any CoP possesses. Books, posters, and displays of teaching materials are (amongst other things) physical traces of the practices of any specific academic discipline, often varying in terms of format or modality but nonetheless straightforward to discern as pertaining to one CoP rather than another. It would not be difficult to distinguish an academic journal paper from psychology on the one hand and from economics on the other: these two PDFs are in a way nothing more than reminders of the decades of work that these two academic disciplines have done to establish themselves whilst also working to distinguish themselves from their neighbours or rivals. Perhaps one department is sufficiently different from its departmental neighbours to constitute a distinct community? Or perhaps the different kinds of work done within a sociology department as compared to a mathematics department helps us to distinguish different communities? The notion that different academic disciplines do things differently is hardly a new one (Becher & Trowler, 2001). Might they therefore be sufficiently distinct so as to constitute CoPs?

But we already have a problem. I am using "department" and "discipline" interchangeably. Here, what I mean to foreground is the notion of an academic subject area – archaeology, economics, film, social policy – which I am taking to be uncontroversial. We can, of course, easily find many examples of departments that are not disciplines, either because they are self-avowedly interdisciplinary (such as an Institute of Advanced Studies – quite a lot of universities have one of these) or because they are, historically, an amalgam of more coherent subject areas (such as Education Studies, my own home, sometimes located in "departments" but at other times in "schools"). But we need to remember that our unit of analysis is not the "department" or the "discipline" but the CoP which, after we have unpacked it from our empirical and theoretical perspective, may correspond to an academic discipline. Or indeed to a department.

In a well-informed account of the different kinds of work done by academics, James (2007) argues that CoPs in universities align to academic disciplines and are to be found clustered around three main areas of activity that characterise – in different ways – the practices of academic staff: research, teaching, and wider departmental practices such as committee meetings, management groups, and so forth. She describes these as being arranged in networks although I suspect that Wenger (1998) might refer to them as *constellations*. Certainly, they are not described as being networks in the sense of being either actor networks or social networks (Jewson, 2007; Latour, 2005). James goes on to argue that members by necessity occupy several sometimes conflicting or contradictory positions, generated through the phenomenon of the person who in one community is an old-timer but in another community is a newcomer. These overlapping forms of membership and participation – easily recognisable to many people reading this book – exemplify the phenomenon described by Wenger (1998) as multimembership. It is in the ways in which these different forms of participation and hence different identities relate and react to each other that complexities in the experience and expertise of "old-timers" in higher education are found. For James, debunking one of the more simplistic criticisms of the CoP model, there is self-evidently no straightforward relationship between biological age, duration of employment, and level of expertise.

Jawitz (2009) likewise focuses on differences in practice. Specifically, he concentrates on the different, overlapping CoPs that are to be found within a single academic setting – a Department of Design – and on the different trajectories that members follow within and across overlapping CoPs. Jawitz (2009, p. 245) contrasts these CoPs with those described in his other research which has covered both social sciences (where he identified two CoPs, one centred on undergraduate teaching and the other on research – which included postgraduate students) and natural sciences (also distributed across two CoPs, the first a research-led CoP, and the second a teaching-focused CoP effectively embedded within the former). In respect of the Department of Design, the arrangement of the CoPs identified is different again. This time, three CoPs are present, and the space between the undergraduate teaching CoP and the postgraduate teaching CoP is bridged by a professional CoP. This third CoP maintains strong links to the design industry that acts as a site of professional activity for several of the academic staff as well as students, illustrating a form of *multimembership* that bridges academic and professional/industrial contexts. For Jawitz, the focus is on the tensions that are to be found between academic identity and professional identity.

James and Jawitz use CoP theory to raise interesting questions relating specifically to staff. Wegner and Nückles (2015) provide a theoretically informed discussion that shifts our attention onto students. Drawing on Lave and Wenger (1991) as well as Wenger (1998), they align CoPs with academic disciplines. Within these disciplinary CoPs, the students are straightforwardly positioned as apprentices. Drawing on Lave and Wenger's (1991) argument that for authentic learning to happen it must take place through LPP whereapprentices must learn through authentic practice and not simply through talking about the practice, Wegner and Nückles foreground the necessity (from a CoP perspective) of the provision of authentic opportunities for students to engage in practice, and to talk about that practice, as a precondition for meaningful learning: "students do not learn something about psychology; instead, they become psychologists" (Wegner & Nückles, 2015, p. 627). At the same time, the lecturers and professors, through their ongoing development of the practice, the discourse, the artefacts and the history of the CoP – that is, the academic discipline – are also continuing to learn.

In discussing the formation of a CoP amongst doctoral students, DeChambeau (2017) draws on several of the paradigmatic components of CoP theory in order to theorise the different ways by which a new cohort of students on a PhD programme in Sustainability Education come together, in both face-to-face and online spaces, drawing on a variety of modes of communication in order to establish a framework for mutual engagement within their discipline. And whilst the joint enterprise of this CoP is self-evident – the doing of the Sustainability Education curriculum – the shared repertoire of the CoP contains some perhaps less-expected elements. One of these (which I found to be of particular interest) was the role played by storytelling amongst members of the community (DeChambeau, 2017, p. 402), which was framed as not only a locus for data construction but also for meaning-making within the CoP, and which in and of itself constitutes an increasingly significant methodology for learning and research in higher education (Mazzoli Smith, 2020).

The three core elements of any CoP – mutual engagement, joint enterprise, and shared repertoire – are explored by Orsmond et al. (2013) in their study of first-, second-, and third-year students in Biological Sciences. Through employing a CoP framework to make sense of the learning that takes place outside the formal curriculum, Orsmond and colleagues foreground relatively mundane but nonetheless important practices such as meeting up outside formal laboratory hours to talk – learning and then drawing on the "talk" of the CoP – about how their work is progressing (mutual engagement), providing peers with copies of useful articles to read (joint enterprise) and discussing project-based assignments and feedback (shared repertoire). As the students progress from the first to the third year of study, these interactions and transactions change to accommodate the different requirements of different stages of engagement in their programmes of study. But they remain as instances of social learning throughout, situated within a CoP that exists alongside the "formal" CoP of the curriculum.

Talking about a locale such as an academic department or a collection of people such as a cohort of undergraduate or doctoral students on the same programme in terms of being CoPs makes sense, not least because we can imagine quite easily how this might work simply through reflecting on different aspects of our own working lives. The idea that a department works as a particular kind of social formation with particular ways of doing things, forms of work, patterns of talking and writing, and so forth is instantly recognisable. If we are to adopt this approach, therefore, it becomes a relatively unproblematic exercise to identify and then do research within or about these and other disciplinary communities, whatever the academic discipline might be: art and design (Shreeve, 2007), teacher education (Tummons, 2008), mathematics (Goodchild et al., 2021), or aviation (O'Brien & Bates, 2015).

But there are, of course, other ways to think about things. Nistor et al. (2015, pp. 259–260) proposed that there are two possible ways to define the boundaries of CoPs within academia more broadly. The first of these aligns with the approach that we have already discussed: of academia being made up of any number of differently sized CoPs with specific discourses, repertoires, practices, and so forth. But the second approach that they have identified is quite different and worth quoting in full: "academia may be seen as a single, large CoP with individuals being able to move within and between different institutions without disrupting their CoP membership, due to a broad understanding of academic practice, and to the increasing internationalization and interdisciplinarity of the academic world" (Nistor et al., 2015, p. 259). At first look, a working definition of a "CoP of academia" such as this surely stretches the elasticity of the theory to the very limit: if we cannot necessarily agree that staff and students can ever be members of the same CoP (Ashwin, 2009), how can we accommodate staff from across the sector as a whole in this way? And yet at the same time, Nistor et al. raise important points around internationalisation and interdisciplinarity (which are issues of particular importance in the contemporary university) that we might easily imagine as elements of practice within and across universities, as facets of joint enterprise self-evidently resting on different patterns of mutual engagement: after all, there is no reason why the joint enterprise of a CoP needs to be restricted to a definition based solely on academic discipline. And so maybe there is more to CoPs than merely disciplines and departments.

Interdisciplinary and Cross-Institutional Communities of Practice

Over the course of the past few months, I have been part of a small working group at my university responsible for setting up a faculty-wide interdisciplinary hub. Hubs such as these are already in place at two other faculties at my university. The idea behind them is to encourage and then provide a home for interdisciplinary programmes of study – new undergraduate or postgraduate programmes that will draw on the expertise of two or more disciplines in order to explore specific themes and problems in new and creative ways. Such cross-pollination of academic disciplines is nothing new, of course, and it is a simple task to find interdisciplinary and multidisciplinary (depending on who you ask, these two constructs are more or less different from each other) curricula on offer at any number of universities, ranging from art and design to environmental humanities. You can even do a course in "interdisciplinary studies" at a small number of places. Interdisciplinarity is an interesting construct for us to think about from a CoP standpoint. By definition, it cuts across the boundaries established by specific academic disciplines and departments, but there is more to it than a simple "pick-and-mix" or "cut-and-shut" approach to curriculum design. An interdisciplinary programme is not only a collection of modules from separate departments that have been assembled in one place: it is a synthesis of historically more or less distinct ways of thinking and working brought to bear on a particular series of intellectual objects and projects. Interdisciplinarity is as much a feature of contemporary universities as are textiles, music, social policy, or geography. It is housed in Institutes of Advanced Studies or similar, which offer courses, run seminar series, welcome visiting scholars, hold writing groups, and so forth – in short, doing all of the things that a "regular" department does, and in a broadly analogous manner. There is no single version of interdisciplinarity insofar as it is a term that can cover a wide array of very different academic projects and interests, and yet at the same time, it is a construct that is clearly identifiable and able to be defined in a relatively straightforward manner. It is, simply put, "a thing".

Things: Reification and Participation

Thinking about "things" happens differently across different academic disciplines. From a CoP perspective, the ways in which things come into being are an important element of how the work of any CoP gets done. CoPs need to not only use but also generate all kinds of stuff in order to function: paper records mean that community members do not have to remember everything; increasingly complex tools allow for more sophisticated operations or measurements; regulations and processes provide order and routine that can aid efficiency; and lanyards and uniforms help community members be identifiable. Engagement in the practices of any CoP relies on having access to and learning how to use any and all such materials, routines, tools, objects, documents, processes, and such like as are required for the CoP to work. Wenger describes the ways in which such stuff comes into being as *reification*. To reify something (it comes from the Latin noun *res* which means "thing" or "matter") is to take something that is in an abstract form and render it in a more explicit or concrete form. Reifications are an essential element of participation, therefore, either because you need to use them (a journal article or a piece of laboratory equipment) or because you need to make new ones (a project report, or a technical drawing). Reification and participation are necessarily intertwined, therefore, and this relationship is described by Wenger as a duality (Wenger, 1998, pp. 68–71).

Back to Interdisciplinary and Cross-Institutional Communities of Practice

It is a pretty simple task to download programme or module specifications for interdisciplinary MA programmes. It is similarly easy to find university departments or institutes that are centred entirely around interdisciplinary studies – addresses, email details for directors of programmes or other affiliated staff, advertisements for seminar series, and so forth. Journals such as *Higher Education Research and Development* and *Studies in Higher Education* have published many articles exploring interdisciplinarity in relation to undergraduates, doctoral students, and staff.

So if we choose to continue breaking down the walls that surround individual academic subjects, we might ask the question: is interdisciplinarity a sufficiently strongly framed construct to sustain a CoP? According to the cross-institutional case study of Pharo et al. (2014), the answer would seem to be that it is. This study, which rests on the practitioner model of CoPs (Wenger et al., 2002), looks at the establishment of what the authors refer to as "*intentional* communities of practice" (Pharo et al., 2014, p. 352; emphasis added) at four different universities in Australia in order to encourage an approach to the teaching of climate change courses on an interdisciplinary basis, through overcoming longer-standing problems such as professional isolation and disciplinary competition that prevent such interdisciplinary collaboration from taking place. The establishment of these CoPs is in turn explicitly linked to the improvement of teaching through the integration of diverse disciplinary perspectives and models of collaborative teaching, with the CoPs in question – one at each university – set up by "activators" and then sustained by "facilitators" who between them occupy clear leadership roles within the CoPs. For Pharo et al., the CoP is not a framework for understanding or enhancing disciplinary-based practices but something very different – a way of overcoming the negative aspects of disciplinary silos.

Relatedly, the study by Buckley and Du Toit (2010), likewise resting on the practitioner model of CoPs, explores cross-institutional approaches to the enhancement of academics' practice across disciplines as part of wider institutional curriculum reform at one university in South Africa. In this study, universities are described as locations primed for the "natural occurrence of CoPs" (Buckley & Du Toit, 2010, p. 494), which require a number of resources in order to flourish: trust, time, opportunities for personal development, and meaningful sharing of knowledge. Universities should encourage the formation of CoPs as vehicles through which collaboration and tacit knowledge sharing can be facilitated. For Buckley and Du Toit, CoPs are informal entities rather than formal structures such as faculty boards or departments.

Themes of internationalisation and cross-institutional work are also picked up by Keay et al. (2014) in their exploration of a project funded by the UK Higher Education Academy (now Advance HE) exploring transnational education (further discussed in May & Keay (2017)). Transnational education is a broad term to describe any institutional arrangement by which students can work towards a credit-bearing module or programme whilst living in a different country from that of the awarding university. Overseas "satellite" campuses, residential schools taught by visiting staff, and franchise arrangements are common and familiar vehicles for such provision. Keay et al. draw on Wenger (1998) in order to explore the ways in which learning and teaching practices within transnational education might be enhanced. Through discussing staff commitment and expertise (joint enterprise), sharing information and mutual help (mutual engagement), and the quality of and access to available resources (shared repertoire), Keay et al. argue for the development of CoPs which "are comprised of academics who have the internationalisation of student learning as their main focus" (May & Keay, 2017, p. 77).

University-wide curriculum reform is also at the heart of the work done by Annala and Mäkinen (2017), this time in Finland. Resting on the academic model of CoPs (Wenger, 1998), Annala and Mäkinen treat the CoP lens as a heuristic model (Lea, 2005), with particular features of CoPs emerging as a consequence of their exploration of the processes of curriculum change over several years at one institution. Annala and Mäkinen (2017, p. 1949) frame their exploration of the complex processes of curriculum reform through reference to mutual engagement (the necessary processes of networking and communication required for the process of curriculum reform), joint enterprise (the shared understanding of the curriculum reform process), and shared repertoire (different traditions and conceptions of curriculum). Firmly situating CoPs as "local disciplinary communities" (Annala & Mäkinen, 2017, p. 1943), the application of these and other elements derived from Wenger (1998) illuminates a number of issues that are both interdisciplinary in the sense that they might be used to explore any process of curriculum renewal and cross-institutional insofar as they might be used to explore curriculum change within different contexts. Curriculum documentation is foregrounded as a key textual artefact, a product of the related processes or duality of participation and reification. For Annala and Mäkinen, through their use of CoP theory, a curriculum document is a reified text, the finalisation of which is pursuant to any number of panel meetings, discussions, consultations, and so forth (curriculum review and refresh processes that many of us will be familiar with) which from a CoP perspective constitute a form of negotiation of meaning (Wenger, 1998, p. 52), reflecting the social and distributed model of learning that CoP theory rests on. This discussion of curriculum provided by Annala and Mäkinen in terms of negotiation of meaning and reification provides an excellent example of how specific elements of CoP theory can be deployed to generate meaningful insights into university practices that we might otherwise take for granted and is worth reflecting on.

Different Ways of Defining Communities of Practice

Up to this point, we have looked at a number of examples from the research literature that have gone about the business of defining CoPs in higher education in one of two ways. The first is in terms of academic disciplines and departments, and the second is in terms of interdisciplinary and cross-institutional initiatives or policies.

The categorisation of an academic discipline or department as a CoP, at first look, makes perfect sense. The idea that a department of historians constitutes a community that is sufficiently distinct from a community of physicists but still sufficiently similar to allow us to consider them both as aspects of a larger whole – a university – seems so obvious as to be not worth describing in too much detail. There are aspects of mutual engagement that are similar: research seminars or tutorials, for example, will be about different things, but will follow particular forms and styles: there will be presentations, PowerPoint slides, and links to the recommended and required reading on the virtual learning environment, and so forth. Other aspects of shared repertoire will be rather more different from each other but still identifiable as being within a particular genre. Both communities (the historians and the physicists) generate textual artefacts – books, assignments, journal papers, funding bids – but these will vary in style and construction as well as content or topic (e.g., members of some academic communities will use the first person in their academic writing whilst others will not). Meantime, the joint enterprises are of course starkly different, reflecting the different academic disciplines at work.

These familiarities or overlaps, which we can scale up in order to consider the other departments that we might find at any individual university, allow us to imagine discipline-based CoPs as being arranged within a larger structure, the whole of which makes up a university. And thinking back to the insights generated by both James (2007) and Wegner and Nückles (2015), through constructing the boundaries of these communities in terms of academic discipline, we can clearly see the objects, practices, and stuff – the reifications – that mark out these boundaries. There are many such reifications: the teaching spaces which vary according to the needs of different academic disciplines; the material resources that are required for work within the discipline; the displays of books, posters, and papers written by members of a department; or the different genres of writing that are inscribed or otherwise manipulated within the discipline. Even how people dress can be seen as a reification of the practices that they engage in. In summary, we could say that because physics departments look, sound, and feel like physics departments and the people who are in them do stuff that looks, reads, and sounds like physics and because history departments look, sound, and feel like history departments and the people who are in them do stuff that looks, reads, and sounds like history, then physics and history are CoPs or, better, disciplinary CoPs.

The alternative is to recognise that we need to think more broadly, outside disciplinary and departmental boundaries, and consider how much of the work that we see getting done in universities happens outside and across subject specialisms, but nonetheless is quite clearly structured in such a way as to constitute a definable form of joint enterprise, contributed to by different members of staff in such a way as to form patterns of mutual engagement, and resourced in such a way as to generate a shared repertoire. And this alternative approach also makes perfect sense. Much of our work as academics takes place outside the strict confines of our academic departments and revolves around assemblages of practice and ways of knowing that are not straightforwardly related to our disciplinary backgrounds. In addition to the interdisciplinary programmes already discussed, we might find university research ethics panels or steering groups for cross-faculty curriculum development and other examples of the kinds of concentrations of activity, focusing on clearly defined tasks and requiring particular forms of engagement, that constitute CoPs. These are not disciplinary CoPs but are nonetheless entirely enrolled in the broader practices of universities and are as straightforwardly recognisable as aspects of higher education as are academic departments.

Universities: Not Just Teachers and Researchers

CoPs are remarkable for their heterogeneity, and researchers have used CoP theory to explore different forms of learning and belonging amongst groups ranging from police officers (Rock, 2005) to the unemployed (Beck, 2007) to nuclear security educators (Moran & Hobbs, 2018). Mindful of this diversity, it seems sensible to assume that universities – also diverse organisations employing lots of different people – could likewise host CoPs that whilst nonetheless displaying a clear alignment to the joint enterprise of the university as a whole – the doing of higher education – would be made up of people, experts as well as apprentices, who are not teaching, research or academic staff, but who are nonetheless central to the practice of these university-bound communities. We might imagine that CoPs are also to be found in a range of professional and administrative contexts. If a call centre can be a CoP (Brannan, 2007), then so can a central admissions office. If radiotherapists working in a medical research company can be a CoP (Swan et al., 2002), then so can ICT technicians working in a humanities faculty.

Academic and teaching staff often do work that does not, at first look, appear to be "academic" work. Lecturers have to chair committees, attend open days, contribute to departmental Boards of Studies meetings, and encourage final-year students to complete the National Student Survey (NSS), alongside their more straightforwardly identifiable teaching and research roles. Then again, attending curriculum review meetings, contributing to moderation events, and writing module handbooks are such necessary aspects of our practice as university teachers that we might argue that they are no more or less vital or necessary to "getting university teaching done" than are the acts of standing up and giving a lecture or moderating a seminar discussion. It seems obvious to include writing feedback and moderating assignments as academic work, so why not also include attending open days, updating content on a virtual learning environment, or liaising with external examiners? Work such as this is as much a part of what we do as is teaching and research.

At the same time there are lots of other people, who are not teaching, research or academic staff, also working in universities and whose work undoubtedly, and necessarily, contributes towards the overall function– the joint enterprise – of the university as a whole (leaving to one side arguments about the exact balance between universities as places of teaching, as places of research, as places for knowledge transfer, as places for nurturing enterprise through monetising invention, and so forth). These people are not occupying primarily academic roles if we confine our notion of academic roles to "just" teaching and research. And yet we have already established that academics always do much more than this. Meanwhile, the professional services, administrative, and ancillary staff (different terminology is used at different institutions) all do work that is necessary for any university to function. The research office staff who help prepare funding bids or ensure that academic staff are complying with institutional and legal requirements for open access publication might easily be imagined as being involved within a community of research practice at some level, and it is impossible to imagine that some forms of research might be done without them. They are not doing the actual work of research – they do not conduct experiments, design survey instruments, or conduct systematic reviews of literature, but they are nonetheless contributing through doing other kinds of work that allow research to happen. The ICT technicians who help prepare online learning materials and the administrative staff who help to populate virtual learning environments might also be seen as being involved in communities of pedagogic practice, working with academic staff as they carry out their teaching. The quality office staff who guide new ideas for programmes of study from initial proposals by a department through to a final curriculum offer via market research, external review, budget allocations, and so forth, are likewise essential. The staff who provide catering and hospitality for when external examiners visit, the solicitors or paralegals who work in human resources departments and advise on appointments, the estates and buildings staff who maintain teaching accommodation, and the porters who help move the furniture in seminar rooms are all contributing work that sustains the university as a whole. The work of the disciplinary and cross-disciplinary CoPs that we discussed above conspicuously relies on people other than academics.

So we need to think about how we might theorise the positions, the *trajectories*, of these members of the university. If we assume that they too are enrolled within disciplinary or cross-disciplinary CoPs, then one way to think about this might be to consider their position in terms of their location in relation to the periphery or the centre of the community. For example, it might be the case that within a disciplinary CoP, the position of an administrator will be somehow more peripheral than the position of a lecturer. Both are involved in the joint enterprise of the community – the actual teaching of modules, courses, and curricula to the students. However, the role of the course lecturer is understood as being closer to the centre because she or he is doing the actual work of teaching, whilst the course administrator does other kinds of work that is still important but less fundamental to the pedagogical exchanges that are central to the community. The administrators know things *about* university teaching (about deadlines for assignments and granting extensions), and they do things that facilitate university teaching (student registration and timetabling), but they do not *do* university teaching – although they are still essential to the work of the discipline overall. Their practices are qualitatively different to those of teaching and research staff, but still focused on the joint enterprise of the CoP: the doing of whatever is needed to get the work of the discipline done.

Alternatively, we might reject any attempt to enrol course administrators and course lecturers in the same CoP, simply because the practices of the course administrators are so different from the practices of the course lecturers. Their respective practices are so distinct that they cannot be members of the same community. Instead, we might put forward the notion that there are two sets or, better, constellations (Wenger, 1998) of CoPs that are closely aligned, both revolving around the central task of teaching. One set of CoPs is that of the lecturers, focusing on university teaching in the broadest sense: the disciplinary and cross-disciplinary CoPs that we have already seen discussed in our examples from the research literature. The second set is that of the administrators: a constellation of administrative CoPs, defined more specifically in relation to the specific areas of student provision that the administrative team is working in, also working in disciplinary or cross-disciplinary ways. The danger is that we end up with a proliferation of CoPs – a collection of CoPs that is so vast that it becomes difficult to keep count of them all, let alone reflect on their practices in order to generate meaningful and useful insights about those very university practices that are of interest to us. A CoP-based inquiry might concentrate on a single department (Herrington et al., 2008), a single area of curriculum provision (Annala & Mäkinen, 2017), a specific group of teachers (Anderson, 2008), or even a single member of academic staff (Arthur, 2016). These CoPs, whatever they are, will all be arrayed in different constellations that may need to be traced, depending on the nature of our inquiry. And we haven't even begun to discuss how we might make room for our students.

Summing Up

Whilst remaining aware of the danger inherent in trying to stretch Communities of Practice theory too far (Tight, 2015), different accounts of higher education practices have identified CoPs in terms of:

- Academic disciplines and departments.
- Interdisciplinary communities, and communities focusing on cross-institutional issues such as internationalisation.
- Communities that include staff and students.
- Separate communities for staff and students.

Conclusion: Making Sense of the Research

In this chapter, we have explored some examples of current and recent literature that have described and/or explained particular aspects of higher education practice through the use of the CoPs framework. Different theoretical and conceptual frameworks catch on to different degrees. Higher education researchers are spoilt for choice when it comes to articles based on Bourdieu, less so for articles based on Lave and Wenger, but in both cases the quality of work published is variable. A further complication when considering CoP theory is found in the differences between the academic and practitioner models. Notwithstanding these questions, we can suggest that thinking about universities as being constituted through different arrangements of CoPs allows us in turn to think about how learning happens, the kinds of resources that learning needs, how everyone working in universities and not "just academics" contribute to teaching, and so forth. We have also introduced a further key theoretical component of CoP theory: the duality of participation and reification. We have not yet spent much time thinking about students, however, and we shall return to them in the next chapter and again in Chapter 7. The key message for now is to recognise the heterogeneity of membership of a CoP and the qualitatively different types of work that can nonetheless be seen as contributing to the joint enterprise of any CoP. In Chapter 4, we shall think some more about how CoPs can be identified but also about how new ones can be encouraged.

References

Anderson, V. (2008). Communities of practice and part-time lecturers: Opportunities and challenges in higher education. In C. Kimble, P. Hildreth, & I. Bourdon (Eds.), *Communities of practice. Creating learning environments for educators* (Vol. 2, pp. 83–103). Information Age Publishing.

Annala, J., & Mäkinen, M. (2017). Communities of practice in higher education: Contradictory narratives of a university-wide curriculum reform. *Studies in Higher Education, 42*(11), 1941–1957.

Arthur, L. (2016). Communities of practice in higher education: Professional learning in an academic career. *International Journal for Academic Development, 21*(3), 230–241.

Ashwin, P. (2009). *Analysing teaching-learning interactions in higher education: Accounting for structure and agency*. Continuum.

Barton, D., & Tusting, K. (Eds.). (2005). *Beyond communities of practice: Language, power and social context*. Cambridge University Press.

Becher, T., & Trowler, P. (2001). *Academic tribes and territories*. Society for Research into Higher Education/Open University Press.

Beck, V. (2007). Unemployment as a community of practice: Tales of survival in the new Germany. In J. Hughes, N. Jewson, & L. Unwin (Eds.), *Communities of practice: Critical perspectives* (pp. 144–155). Routledge.

Brannan, M. J. (2007). Sexuality, gender and legitimate peripheral participation. In J. Hughes, N. Jewson, & L. Unwin (Eds.), *Communities of practice: Critical perspectives* (pp. 120–130). Routledge.

Buckley, S., & Du Toit, A. (2010). Academics leave your ivory tower: Form communities of practice. *Educational Studies, 36*(5), 493–503.

DeChambeau, A. (2017). The practice of being a student: CoPs and graduate student success. In J. McDonald, & A. Cater-Steel (Eds.), *Implementing communities of practice in higher education* (pp. 395–422). Springer Nature.

Goodchild, S., Apkarian, N., Rasmussen, C., & Katz, B. (2021). Critical stance within a community of inquiry in an advanced mathematics course for pre-service teachers. *Journal of Mathematics Teacher Education, 24*(3), 231–252.

Herrington, M., Kendall, A., Hughes, J., Lacey, C., Smith, R., Dye, V., Baig, R., & O'Leary, M. (2008). Space, resistance and identities: University-based teacher educators developing a community of practice. In C. Kimble, P. Hildreth, & I. Bourdon (Eds.), *Communities of practice. Creating learning environments for educators* (Vol. 2, pp. 191–212). Information Age Publishing.

James, N. (2007). The learning trajectory of 'old-timers': Academic identities and communities of practice in higher education. In J. Hughes, N. Jewson, & L. Unwin (Eds.), *Communities of practice: Critical perspectives* (pp. 131–143). Routledge.

Jawitz, J. (2009). Academic identities and communities of practice in a professional discipline. *Teaching in Higher Education, 14*(3), 241–251.

Jewson, N. (2007). Cultivating network analysis: Rethinking the concept of 'community' within 'communities of practice. In J. Hughes, N. Jewson, & L. Unwin (Eds.), *Communities of practice: Critical perspectives* (pp. 68–82). Routledge.

Keay, J., May, H., & O' Mahony, J. (2014). Improving learning and teaching in transnational education: Can communities of practice help? *Journal of Education for Teaching, 40*(3), 251–266.

Lang, I., & Canning, R. (2010). The use of citations in educational research: The instance of the concept of 'situated learning. *Journal of Further and Higher Education, 34*(2), 291–301.

Latour, B. (2005). *Reassembling the social: An introduction to actor-network theory.* Clarendon Press.

Lave, J., & Wenger, E. (1991). *Situated learning: Legitimate peripheral participation.* Cambridge University Press.

Lea, M. (2005). Communities of practice' in higher education: Useful heuristic or educational model? In D. Barton, & K. Tusting (Eds.), *Beyond communities of practice: Language, power and social context* (pp. 180–197). Cambridge University Press.

May, H., & Keay, J. (2017). Using communities of practice to internationalise higher education: Practical and strategic considerations. In J. McDonald, & A. Cater-Steel (Eds.), *Communities of practice: Facilitating social learning in higher education* (pp. 73–98). Springer Nature.

Mazzoli Smith, L. (2020). Diversifying the discourse of progression to higher education: Digital storytelling methodology in widening participation practice. *Widening Participation and Lifelong Learning, 22*(1), 79–94.

Moran, M., & Hobbs, C. (2018). From communities of interest to communities of practice: The role and impact of professional development in nuclear security education. *British Journal of Education Studies, 66*(1), 87–107.

Nistor, N., Daxecker, I., Stanciu, D., & Diekamp, O. (2015). Sense of community in academic communities of practice: Predictors and effects. *Higher Education, 69*(2), 257–273.

O'Brien, W., & Bates, P. (2015). Looking and feeling the part: Developing aviation students' professional identity through a community of practice. *Teaching in Higher Education, 20*(8), 821–832.

Orsmond, P., Merry, S., & Callaghan, A. (2013). Communities of practice and ways to learning: Charting the progress of biology undergraduates. *Studies in Higher Education, 38*(6), 890–906.

Pharo, E., Davison, A., McGregor, H., Warr, K., & Brown, P. (2014). Using communities of practice to enhance interdisciplinary teaching: Lessons from four Australian Institutions. *Higher Education Research and Development, 33*(2), 341–354.

Rock, F. (2005). 'I've picked some up from a colleague': Language, sharing and communities of practice in an institutional setting. In D. Barton, & K. Tusting (Eds.), *Beyond communities of practice: Language, power and social context*. Cambridge University Press.

Shreeve, A. (2007). Learning development and study support: An embedded approach through communities of practice. *Art, Design and Communication in Higher Education*, 6(1), 11–25.

Swan, J., Scarbrough, H., & Robertson, M. (2002). The construction of communities of practice in the management of innovation. *Management Learning*, 33(4), 477–496.

Thomas, G. (2007). *Education and theory: Strangers in paradigms*. Open University Press.

Tight, M. (2015). Theory application in higher education research: The case of communities of practice. *European Journal of Higher Education*, 5(2), 111–126.

Tummons, J. (2008). Assessment, and the literacy practices of trainee PCET teachers. *International Journal of Educational Research*, 47(3), 184–191.

Tummons, J. (2018). *Learning architectures in higher education: Beyond communities of practice*. Bloomsbury.

Wegner, E., & Nückles, M. (2015). Knowledge acquisition or participation in communities of practice? Academics' metaphors of teaching and learning at the university. *Studies in Higher Education*, 40(4), 624–643.

Wenger, E. (1998). *Communities of practice: Learning, meaning and identity*. Cambridge University Press.

Wenger, E., McDermott, R., & Snyder, W. (2002). *Cultivating communities of practice*. Harvard Business School Press.

Chapter 4

Setting Up a Learning Architecture

Introduction

In this chapter, I discuss Wenger's notion of the Learning Architecture: the blueprint for a Community of Practice (CoP). The Learning Architecture framework outlines the process through which new Communities of Practice can be developed and then encouraged within formal pedagogical settings such as universities – although it is important to remember that how this CoP will subsequently work cannot be straightforwardly predicted or guaranteed. In discussing the constituent elements of a Learning Architecture, I will draw on several of the theoretical components outlined in Chapters 1–3, and also introduce a small number of additional ones. Through this discussion, I will explore the ways in which Wenger proposes that a CoP can be encouraged into being within the context of any formal educational establishment.

The Pedagogy Problem

CoPs change over time: sometimes they change rapidly and in drastic ways; at other times, the pace of change is very slow. The dynamism that is inherent in any CoP, irrespective of the speed of change, helps us to explain how new practices, new ways of knowing, new bodies of knowledge, new tools and artefacts, and so forth all come into being. Appropriately enough, Communities of Practice theory has also changed over time, with the somewhat impressionistic idea of the CoP as proposed by Lave and Wenger (1991) overtaken to by the richly detailed model detailed by Wenger (1998). The focus of the earlier book is apprenticeship learning through Legitimate Peripheral Participation (LPP): the CoP becomes the focus for inquiry in the later work. However, not long after we have got to grips with the richly detailed academic model of the CoP, Wenger shifts focus once again. The practitioner model foreshadowed in Wenger (2000) and then detailed more fully in Wenger et al. (2002) takes the CoP away from the academic world and into the world of businesses and organisations, of organisational learning and knowledge management. Meanwhile, other researchers and writers have contributed to the discussion, resolving perceived problems within CoP theory and offering different solutions (Chaiklin & Lave, 1996; Kirshner & Whitson, 1997; Wertsch et al., 1995).

The CoP problem (as it were) that needs to be resolved more than any other, for the purposes of the argument that I am making in this book, relates to the extent to which the provision of education and training in any formal institutional context might be made sense of. As we have already seen, there are many articles, chapters, and so forth within educational research that have used CoP theory. But this is despite the central fact that the idea of any kind of mode of instruction – of pedagogy – is anathema to the arguments made by Lave and Wenger:

> In a community of practice, there are no special forms of discourse aimed at apprentices or crucial to their centripetal movement toward full participation that correspond to the marked genres of the question-answer-evaluation format of classroom teaching, or the lecturing of college professors or midwife-training course instructors.
> (Lave & Wenger, 1991, p. 108)

Any learner – whether they are an apprentice or an old-timer – cannot learn more about the practice that they wish to engage with only by talking about it in an "education and training" kind of a way. By this I mean to foreground what is arguably the key insight proposed by Lave and Wenger: if you take an authentic practice and try to package it up into an educational format, which by definition means that you have to transport a particular kind of practice away from its everyday context and into a formal pedagogical environment, then what you are engaging with is not the authentic practice, but an "educational" version of it, and these are not the same. The practice, once transported from its original context, would lose its authenticity. Without authenticity, there can be no legitimacy. And, consequently, there can be no LPP, no learning.

For example, imagine studying physics at school. No matter how well equipped the classrooms, how well qualified the teachers, or how well motivated the students, this CoP will be a CoP of "school physics", not of "physicists":

> …there are vast differences between the ways high school physics students participate in and give meaning to their activity and the way professional physicists do.
> (Lave & Wenger, 1991, p. 99)

Now, this does not stop us from exploring schools (or, indeed, universities) as CoPs – it simply means that we have to be careful when defining what those CoPs actually are about and what they are doing. The examples of situated learning that Lave and Wenger (1991) describe are all situated within authentic contexts of practice: tailors in Liberia (Lave's own ethnographic research); midwives in Mexico; quartermasters in the US Navy; and butchers in US supermarkets. In these instances, learning through LPP is happening in and through practice and this is what generates authenticity. A school is a very particular kind of social setting or context, and, of course, learning will be happening within a school in just the same way – through social practice – as it will be happening in a tailor's workshop. But what is being practiced and therefore learned needs to be carefully defined and described. In a school, it is "school versions" of things that are being practiced. Schools are particular kinds of sociocultural settings – particular kinds of CoPs – and what is also being learned is "how to be at school" (Lave & Wenger, 1991). Universities are also particular kinds of sociocultural settings. They are constellations of CoPs made up of particular ways of doing things, of talking, of making stuff, and so forth. If a tailor's workshop or an insurance claims centre can be explored from an anthropological standpoint in order to describe and make sense of the practices of learning that are to be found within them, then it is not unreasonable to assume that a physics department or a social sciences institute can be similarly explored – just as we have done in Chapters 1–3 of this book.

If we are going to describe universities as CoPs, we need to resolve the pedagogy problem, therefore – to find a way to explain how a formal language of teaching can be inserted into the design of a sociocultural formation that rests on an authentic discourse of participation, not an artificial discourse of instruction. And we need to do this in order to make sense of an obvious problem with CoP theory as originally constituted: can all the things that people learn be explained in terms of CoP membership? Can the authentic situated learning that characterises the apprenticeship of the tailor's workshop also explain how people become surgeons or architects? In an early critique of CoPs and situated learning, Jay Lemke (1997) suggested that in order to explain and describe more complex learning processes, a different arrangement of CoPs would be needed. It is simply insufficient, he argued, to propose that some particular bodies of knowing and expertise could be acquired and utilised simply by sharing a sociocultural space with more experienced elders. Some ways of knowing require more formalised instruction. Therefore, in order to participate in some CoPs where the practice is particularly complex, prior membership of another CoP is needed as a prerequisite. Successful participation in this first CoP would then allow access to the second. Lemke's theoretical innovation allows us to make sense of CoPs within educational settings. Joining a CoP of architects rests on prior membership of a CoP of "architect education"; membership of a "medical education" CoP in turn allows for participation in a CoP of medical practitioners; historians go through membership of "historian education" CoPs before "becoming" historians. These "education" CoPs (as it were), such as those discussed in Chapter 3, are all therefore constituted in such a way that successful passage through them in turn allows access to other, related, CoPs. The successful negotiation of passage through a disciplinary CoP such as that found in a history department would therefore afford access to the CoP of doing history and being a historian. This does not mean that all history students have to choose to become historians rather than choosing careers in accountancy, law, or teaching (all three of which are popular choices for history graduates); nor does it mean that the only way to become an historian is to have studied history at university. But the alignment between the two CoPs – one of "historian education" and one of "doing history and being an historian" is so close that the border between them is easy to navigate (and we shall return to this in Chapter 6).

Learning Architectures

The *Communities of Practice* book is very much situated in the world of work, however, not of education. Wenger's ethnographic research is situated within a medical insurance claims processing centre, and the different forms of learning, of participation, of knowing, and so forth that he describes pertain to this specific organisational context, rather than to the world of formal, institutional education that we are preoccupied with. Nonetheless, Wenger sets out for the first time a series of statements as to how the insights generated through the broader discussion of social learning and LPP within CoPs might be applied to formal educational contexts (Wenger, 1998, pp. 223–278). In doing this, he challenges head-on the refutations of formal pedagogy and schooling found within the earlier book (Lave & Wenger, 1991, pp. 99–100, 107–108). This series of statements outlines a step-by-step process through which a series of materials and resources can be brought together in such a way as to encourage the development of a CoP. This collection of materials and resources is described as a Learning Architecture. Simply put, a Learning Architecture is the term that we use, within the world of CoP theory, to describe all of the stuff that we need to set up a module or programme of study – resources, buildings, people, routines, assessment tasks, books, learning and teaching strategies, and anything else that we might need and that we anticipate, thanks to our theoretical standpoint, as being situated within a CoP.

A Learning Architecture is not just an inventory for a course design; however, it is also the solution to the pedagogy problem within CoP theory. It is a framework for designing for learning. More specifically, it is a framework for designing a potential series of sociocultural, physical, and online, where particular opportunities for learning through engaging in practice are made available to all of the people who are within that space. It is impossible to build a CoP from scratch because that is not how they work. CoPs are emergent and organic sociocultural entities. The Learning Architecture provides the infrastructure around and through which a CoP can come into being.

A full explanation of why Learning Architectures work in the way that they do requires a discussion of those aspects of CoP theory that underpin them, and I shall return to this momentarily. For now, it is sufficient to note the components of a Learning Architecture – which in fact will be entirely familiar to many, if not all, of the readers of this book – from a more everyday and practical standpoint. For convenience, we can split them into three categories – although they all overlap in practice. First, we have material or physical resources: workshop tools, stools and chairs, data projectors and tablet PCs, graph paper, pencils, books, PDF files, and so forth. In a way, we can include people in this category as well, and this will include lecturers and librarians, technicians, and professional services staff as well as visitors (guest lecturers and ambassadors for placements), employers (e.g., for students on professional courses), external examiners, and open day representatives (who need to let you into the CoP in the first place). Second, we have immaterial or non-physical resources: routines, attitudes, and feelings. For example, a student on a social work postgraduate course will need to develop and embody an *ethic* of care and professionalism as much as a theoretical understanding of those same things. Third, we have processes and procedures: teaching, assessment, demonstrations, moderation meetings, placements, admissions, tutorials, assessment boards, and so forth – any kind of habitual, routinised form of activity, which will both require and allow use of different kinds of material or physical resources and different kinds of non-physical resources as well. All of these objects, people, routines, and so forth all constitute a Learning Architecture.

The Conceptual Foundations of a Learning Architecture

By now, we have a good sense of social theories of learning in general, and of how a particular form of learning for newcomers or apprentices (LPP) is to be found within CoPs. We also have a developing understanding of how, if we want to design an environment for some planned or intended learning to happen although we cannot predict that learning will happen in the way that we might intend, we can assemble a Learning Architecture. The final stage in this part of our inquiry, therefore, is to consider the theoretical underpinnings of the Learning Architecture, of which there are four different parts. Each part draws on different elements of CoP theory more generally: some of these have been discussed already, whereas others will be new to us. The four conceptual parts of a Learning Architecture rest on a series of dualisms, as follows:

1 Reification and Participation
2 Designed and Emergent
3 Local and Global
4 Identification and Negotiability

Once again, it is important to note that these theoretical dualisms are interrelated and work equally to support a Learning Architecture – no one dualism is more important than any other.

1 Reification and Participation

Social theories of learning rest on a number of core assumptions: one of these is that learning involves the whole person. From a sociocultural perspective, learning is not simply a cognitive process but a process involving knowing in doing things, talking with people, trying things out, and both seeing how things work or are done and being allowed to do those same things. It involves the whole person. When new members begin to learn the practices of a community, they will require opportunities to take part in the authentic practice of the community: to participate firstly at a peripheral level and then more fully over time and as expertise is developed. New undergraduate students do not undertake independent research projects straight away. Instead, they work on more discrete, situated topics and gradually build up expertise in their subject. By the time they get to their third year of study, they have become sufficiently immersed in their disciplinary expertise – and also in the ways in which research is conducted within their disciplines – that they are ready to undertake their "capstone" projects (Jawitz, 2007). The learning of the new students – the newcomers to the CoP – is not only characterised by participation – by doing things, however, but also by making things, by having a concrete impact on the practices at hand, even if only peripherally – and this is another example of reification (Wenger, 1998). Sociology students will write assignments, mathematics students will write code, and teacher education students and fine arts students will both create portfolios, although these will of course be made up of very different items and objects. As well as bringing new reifications into being, students will also draw on existing reifications such as journal articles, module handbooks, websites, and seminars. Being a student – participating in the CoP – involves both using existing reifications and generating new ones. Reification and participation always go together; therefore, practice (which always involves learning) leads to the use and/or creation of things, objects, and all kinds of other stuff that encapsulate, make visible, allow, help, and make (more or less) permanent the practices being done within that the community: participation always involves reification, and reifications are brought into use during participation.

The relationship between reification and participation focuses our attention, therefore, on the balance that has to be established to allow apprentices or newcomers firstly to come to know about, use or otherwise draw on the existing tools, objects, and artefacts of a community, and secondly to amend, add to, edit, or reconfigure these same tools and objects, and to use them to create, shape, or alter other things as well. It is through a process of *negotiation* (Wenger, 1998, p. 264) between participation and reification that people are able to engage in practice and therefore able to learn. If the newcomer is provided only with opportunities for participation that do not include reification, then the learning that is afforded becomes illegitimate. This is because, without reification, participation – and therefore learning – cannot be authentic. English students need to read the set texts, discuss them in seminars, write about them in their essays, and then read their feedback. Sport and Exercise Science students need to not only learn about the physiological and anatomical functions of different parts of the human body during seminars but also how to measure them during laboratory sessions and then record the measurements in the correct format. For authentic learning to happen, students need to be able to engage in the authentic practices of the CoP. This *mutual engagement* requires access to the full array of resources of the community, including opportunities to not only utilise these resources but also add to them.

2 Designed and Emergent

A social model of learning tells us that learning in a CoP is a fluid, complex, and possibly also troublesome phenomenon. It cannot be predicted or straightforwardly itemised on a checklist. It is possible to specify some of the background conditions that are required for learning to happen (access to authentic practice, acceptance by and guidance from acknowledged expert practitioners, availability of appropriate materials, routines, and tools), but it is not possible to specify *exactly* what will be learned – only that learning will be taking place as a consequence of participation. Consequently, the design of any Learning Architecture has to be mindful of the different ways in which students will go about the "work" of learning. Learning usually requires effort and application, but it can also be unanticipated and even accidental, irrespective of what it is that is being learned, or where the learning is taking place. This work will include how the newcomers talk about and work with the resources provided, the ways in which different lecturers interact with their students, the correct ways in which the resources, processes, tools, or materials have to be employed, and so on. Things such as these all make a difference to how learning happens – that is, to the experience of participation (of LPP for the newcomers specifically) within the CoP.

When designing a Learning Architecture we can anticipate, to a high degree of appropriateness and accuracy (derived from our own knowing, our own academic and professional histories or trajectories, and the expertise and experience gathered during our own time served within either this or other, related CoPs), the stuff that we, as university teachers, might need. This includes the reifications that we create for use with our students (module handbooks and slide decks, seminar and laboratory activities, formative and/or practice tasks, and so forth) as well as those which come from outside (new workshop or laboratory equipment, new e-books for the library, and so forth). All of these components are part of the design for the Learning Architecture, and these are elements that can be listed, audited, and even put on a checklist. However, they cannot be straightforwardly or unproblematically evaluated. We can never know exactly how different students will react to our choice of activities, our experiments or our lectures, from one year to the next. Each student is an individual, enfolded within an individual biography and history that impacts their learning as they travel along their unique trajectory within the CoP. Consequently, the nature of their participation is similarly unique, although it may well be the case that the trajectories of a cohort of students, considered as a group, and the natures of their respective participations are very closely aligned and are very similar in lots of ways. That is to say, a cohort of students will follow trajectories that are very similar and closely aligned, but each trajectory will nonetheless be unique. Nor is it the case that just because students participate, they do so in ways exactly determined by staff. As university teachers, we cannot always anticipate which questions will provoke discussion and which will fall flat, which procedures will be easy to adopt, and which will need more practice. We have established that learning is an emergent process and teaching is just one of the structuring resources that newcomers might use. But what matters here is not a focus on how teaching impacts learning – because it is hard, if not impossible, to directly link the two – but rather, how teaching and learning can "interact so as to become structuring resources for each other" (Wenger, 1998, p. 267). A focus on Learning Architecture allows us to focus on the relationship between teaching, which is designed, and learning, which is emergent. Practice – and, therefore, learning – is not the *result* of design, but an emergent *response* to it.

3 Local and Global

At this point, we can be confident in saying that CoPs do not exist in isolation: earlier references to boundaries and constellations have hinted at the more extensive discussion of relationships between CoPs that we will return to in more depth in Chapter 6. For now, it is sufficient to understand that arrangements of CoPs – sometimes of CoPs that have lots in common and at other times of CoPs that are very different from each other – exist in such a way as to allow for the movement of both people (teachers, students, examiners, technicians) and things (tools, habits, texts, and machines) between them. Nor is any CoP entirely homegrown or indigenous in its culture. Tracing the history of any CoP will indicate links to others. These might be CoPs that are now defunct but that have left behind traces in the practices of a current one, or extant CoPs that have shaped the formation of a current one, perhaps by contributing to a Learning Architecture. An account of any CoP, therefore, will need in some way to at least acknowledge the ways in which the practices of that community are shared with or borrowed from another one. This will, of course, vary according to the nature, proximity, and intensity of the relationships between them. Sometimes, a CoP will have a close relationship with a neighbour or set of neighbours, allowing members and materials to cross the boundaries between them in a straightforward manner. At other times, however, *boundary crossing* might be restricted or even discouraged. The links from one community to another can be plentiful and obvious, or minimal and difficult to identify, but they are always present. Traces of these links might be found in how community members talk, particular activities that the community might encourage or discourage, how tools and artefacts have been built or used, and so forth. Or, to put it another way, we can say that every CoP consists of elements that are both *local* (that is to say, native or indigenous) and *global* (that is, borrowed, donated, appropriated, or shared from another CoP or group of CoPs).

The relationship between the global and the local can be mapped out in all kinds of ways. Some of these balances can be considered in terms of the balance of influence or power between different communities. For example, degree programmes are often mapped onto a professional standards framework so that a specific endorsement or process of accreditation overseen by a relevant trade or professional body might be made available to students on successful completion of the programme: programmes as diverse as psychology, pharmacy, social work, and podiatry are often designed in such a way as to be aligned to relevant professional standards and can also lead to automatic professional registration after graduation. Another way in which ideas and influences from one CoP can travel to another can be found in external examining or reviewing. External examiners and reviewers can provide insights from the wider landscape of practices, across the HE sector as a whole, that might be applied at the local departmental or institutional level. Placements allow for a very different kind of traffic between CoPs, centred on students rather than staff. In ways such as these, the relationship between the global and the local is accomplished through the movement of both people and things across different kinds of geographical, institutional, and organisational boundaries. It might not always be necessary to trace those networks through which the global impacts on the local, or along which the local reports back to the global, but if they are to form a focus for inquiry, then we need to be mindful of how they are constituted in terms of the relationships between the people and the staff who make up the constellation. How far and how fast they can travel, how successfully they travel, or what happens at the end of the journey, may all need to be accounted for.

4 Identification and Negotiability

Identity is a further important aspect of membership (and therefore of learning as well) within any CoP. When newcomers begin to engage in practice through LPP – in the enterprise of the community, working with or creating reifications, learning the talk or discourse of the community – they also begin to build/add to their identities as students, perhaps with a particular interest in one subject area or another. At the same time, the CoP adjusts slightly around the newcomers, as the other members come to know who the newcomers are and to acknowledge their identities as peripheral members at first and as fuller members over time. Identity work is both an inward-looking process as the newcomers (re)construct their senses of selves, and an outward-facing process, as the newcomers become recognised within the CoP. Some aspects of identity are easy to notice, for example, the wearing of a t-shirt or hooded top decorated with a departmental logo, or the wearing of an identity or library card in a lanyard. Other aspects of identity take a little more effort to identify, such as how people talk or write differently depending on their academic discipline.

Identity needs to be understood in terms of both the person and the context in which they are situated. It is a product of an ongoing series of interactions between any member of the CoP in question, and the CoP that they are a member of. Some aspects of practice have to be followed quite closely – such as using particular academic conventions when writing assignments. Other aspects of practice are not so closely monitored – such as whether to wear a library card in a lanyard or carry it in a mobile phone case. Some aspects of practice are fixed and unmoveable – such as having to study a core module. Others are more fluid – such as being able to choose assessment topics and/or formats. This two-way process is referred to as *negotiation*, which is the capacity to "shape the meanings that matter within a social configuration" (Wenger, 1998, p. 197). That is to say, it is through being able to contribute to the actions, discussions, or reifications of the CoP in a meaningful way, that participation is not only engaged but also deepened. Such meaning-making always relies on the trajectory and position of the participant; however, a newcomer often cannot modify or control the meanings that are being negotiated to the same degree as an old-timer. Nonetheless, negotiation is always present.

If a CoP is going to thrive (which is by no means guaranteed – communities always have to work to sustain themselves), it needs to allow all of the members to reconcile the need to match up to the requirements or standards of the community on the one hand, with the ability and opportunity to act independently within it on the other. If students feel powerless or ignored within a particular CoP, then they will become alienated from it and consequently will not feel able or willing to participate and, as a result, will not be able to learn. If, however, learners are able to make some kind of choice or informed input regarding aspects of their practice, then their participation, and hence their learning, will be deeper and more meaningful. Therefore, a balance needs to be struck regarding the extent to which members identify with the practices, goals, or aspirations of a community, and the extent to which members can negotiate aspects of their practice. The CoP needs to establish a balance between identity and negotiation in order to function, and this involves all of the members of the community (newcomers and old-timers) engaging in two different – but complementary – modes of work (Wenger, 1998, p. 220): *identification* work, and *participation* work. Identification work describes those ways in which people work to help others feel part of a community, as well as establishing themselves as members, and requires things from individual members such as acceptance of habits and rules, making a commitment to the community, and such like. Participation work describes those ways in which members not only engage in the practice of the community but also build their relationships with other members and requires things such as listening to other perspectives, sharing resources, coming to a consensus, managing confrontation, compromise, and so forth.

The Practice of "Teaching"

In 1997, the Dearing Report into Higher Education was published. This government-commissioned report into the contemporary state of UK Higher Education emerged from an inquiry chaired by Ronald Dearing who was then chancellor of Nottingham University. Amongst the many recommendations proposed for the improvement of higher education (HE) provision was a greater focus on university teaching, including the establishment of an Institute for Learning and Teaching in Higher Education, which later became the HE Academy and then Advance HE. The period after Dearing saw serious conversations about the nature of teaching enter HE for the first time. Arguments such as whether teaching is an "art" or a "science", whether or not teachers should be "instructors" or "facilitators" or whether teaching should focus more on "content" or on "participation" are by now well established in research literature. Irrespective of the definitions or philosophies of teaching that we might hold to, the practice of teaching is understood as being complex and diverse (Jarvis, 2006). If it is relatively simple to say what teaching is, it is not quite so simple to say what teaching does, and the relationship (or lack thereof) between teaching and learning remains a matter of debate (Case, 2015). Nonetheless, "teaching" as a social practice is an undeniable element of what goes on in a university. As university teachers, we explain concepts and procedures to our students, generate reading lists and module handbooks, describe and discuss different aspects of our courses, and encourage and motivate our students. We ask and answer questions, provide feedback on assignments, and show our students how to do the stuff that they need to do.

From the perspective of CoP theory, we can argue that teaching is a form of practice that is always found – albeit in differing ways – within any university-based CoP. It is separate from learning, but they are nonetheless related. Or, as Wenger puts it, "learning is an emergent, ongoing process, *which may use teaching as one of its many structuring resources*" (Wenger, 1998, p. 267, emphasis added). Within a CoP, teaching is just one of the resources that helps learning happen just as a journal article or a laboratory procedure or a field site visit helps learning happen. From this perspective, teaching becomes part of the shared repertoire of the CoP. Therefore, just like any other element of shared repertoire within any CoP, teaching is a cultural tool that can be utilised by those members of the community who have the appropriate expertise to use it: the teachers. Wenger concludes that *"teaching does not cause learning*: what ends up being taught may or may not be what was taught, or more generally what the institutional organisation of instruction intended" (Wenger, 1998, p. 267, emphasis added). That is to say, teaching no more directly causes learning to happen than does the provision of a set of tools, or a series of instructional manuals. Nor can we isolate the teaching from the other elements of the architecture – it is an integral part of the CoP, just as learning is. If we recall that teaching is just one of several structuring resources within a CoP, then the emphasis shifts from the teacher to the student, who will have to do effortful work of learning within the CoP in order to travel along their chosen and/or required trajectories (as discussed in Chapter 2). Learning takes work and requires active engagement by the student – the newcomer – with all of the structuring resources at their disposal. These resources include, but are by no means restricted to, teaching.

Putting It All Together: From Designing a Module to Designing a Learning Architecture

Having the freedom to shape our own curricula, to write new modules and programmes that reflect not only our research interests but also our educational philosophies, is one of the great privileges of working as a university teacher. This is not to say that we can simply teach whatever we like. Our ideas for new modules and degree schemes are modulated by a variety of factors such as the requirements of professional bodies, the opinions of external examiners; the commercial imperatives of the institutions that we work for; or contemporary intellectual trends or paradigms. Mindful of drivers such as these, module and/or programme design is a commonplace task for many of us in higher education. Some of us will undoubtedly spend much of our time working with a curriculum that has been provided for us and that leaves relatively little room for flexibility or customisation: our job is to interpret and then "deliver" those modules that we are responsible for. Others of us will be required to draw up much more detailed schema, perhaps even to design entire modules and programmes for the purposes of validation. And sometimes our work will involve a bit of both. For anyone with responsibilities for designing and/or implementing a curriculum, there are three needs that must be met if students are going to be able to participate and, therefore, to be able to learn. These are described by Wenger as follows (Wenger, 1998, p. 271):

1 Places of engagement.
2 Materials and experiences with which to build an image of the world and themselves.
3 Ways of having an effect on the world and making their actions matter.

None of these needs are, in and of themselves, novel or unexpected. Even the newest university lecturer, freshly appointed after completing a PhD, is aware of the importance of appropriate teaching accommodation, fitted out with the right equipment and resources so that the students are able to experience an authentic sample of what the "real world" of the discipline that they are learning will look and feel like. The notion that a greater familiarity with the materials, resources, and artefacts that pertain to the discipline will help students build confidence, as well as expertise, is similarly unsurprising. And there can be few students who would happily agree to performing tasks or practising techniques that did not in some way align with the authentic world of the discipline within which they imagine themselves becoming increasingly absorbed. Or, to put it another way, just as CoPs are already present in universities (as we discussed in Chapter 1), it is the case that many aspects of Learning Architectures are also already present. Our job is to identify what's there so that we can plug any gaps, and use CoP theory to explain how and why the Learning Architecture will work in the way that it does.

Empirical and Conceptual Accounts of Learning Architectures in Higher Education

In comparison to some of the other theoretical components of Wenger's book, it is unambiguously the case that Learning Architectures are both under-explored and under-used, and I for one am at a loss to explain why this might be, although the extent to which different theories get used (or not) within educational research seems somewhat arbitrary, and often is not straightforwardly connected to the value, rigour, or appropriateness of the theory in question (Tight, 2018). Nonetheless, a small number of research articles have been published that foreground the Learning Architecture framework in useful ways within HE. Interestingly, different forms of online learning provision provide a common focus. An empirical paper by Brosnan and Burgess (2003) explores the provision of continuing professional development within social care – a two-stage CPD programme consisting of initial face-to-face provision followed by an online component. Drawing on interviews with and online discussions between programme participants, Brosnan and Burgess use the Learning Architecture framework to evaluate the CPD provision as an online CoP. Sorensen and Ó Murchú (2004) likewise focus on online provision and use the four dualisms (described above) that underpin a Learning Architecture to describe two distinct curricula: the first is a qualitative research methodologies course; the second is an online learning course. Sorensen and Ó Murchú draw out common features across these two programmes of study that foreground the importance of student-centred approaches to course and curriculum design. A paper by McLoughlin et al. (2008) investigates peer mentoring to help support placement learning for graduate students on a Diploma in Education course. Having used the Learning Architecture framework to establish an online CoP, McLoughlin and colleagues analyse the online interactions of the Diploma students in order to describe the online CoP in terms of mutual engagement, joint enterprise, and shared repertoire. In a conceptual paper by Cousin and Deepwell (2005), the role of CoPs in facilitating networked learning is discussed through the establishment of a Learning Architecture "which can enable rich forms of learner participation" (Cousin & Deepwell, 2005, p. 63). These papers, alongside others that explore Learning Architectures in trade union education (Creanor & Walker, 2005), early years education and primary schooling (Smith, 2009), and educational leadership in schools (Scanlan, 2012), provide examples of theoretically informed research that illustrates the explanatory potential of CoP theory through careful accounts of how CoPs can be brought into being.

Summing Up: Engendering Communities of Practice

In order to encourage CoPs, we need to establish Learning Architectures that meet a number of conditions:

- A Learning Architecture is nothing more than the entire infrastructure – of people, resources, and places – that a CoP requires. This may include lecture rooms, workbenches, assessments, websites, technicians, lecturers, books, tools, portfolios, guest speakers, placements – anything, in fact, that is needed.
- Any deficit in the authenticity of the Learning Architecture will always, necessarily, impact the authenticity of the learning that will emerge.
- A CoP cannot be specified in advance, nor can the behaviour of a CoP be predicted; however, a Learning Architecture can be specified in advance.
- A CoP is never isolated: it is always in connection with, and overlapping with, other CoPs. As such, some elements of the Learning Architecture – and therefore the CoP in turn – will always come from outside.
- Once the CoP is established, it is not possible to predict exactly what learning will happen, when, and in what order. It is possible to establish a broadly generalisable account of the learning that will take place, but there will always be unanticipated variation due to the emergent nature of learning.
- The emergent nature of learning within a CoP means that there is no "right" way through which learning might happen. Or, to put it another way, there is no causal link between teaching and learning. Learning relies equally on all of the resources of the CoP, not just one of them (whether it is teaching or whether it is something else such as a journal article or YouTube video). Teaching is just one element of a Learning Architecture that can be specified as one of the planned resources.

Conclusion: Learning Architectures and Communities of Practice

"Learning Architecture" is at one level nothing more than the CoP way of describing the list of all of the things that are needed for a programme of study. Whether this is an entire degree scheme or an individual module will depend on the specificities of our jobs, what we are doing or being asked to do. If we are writing a new module, then we'll need a module specification and a student handbook, teaching rooms, appropriately qualified and expert staff, laboratory and/or library resources, access to transport if we need field trips, journal subscriptions, and so on. When we describe this assemblage as a "Learning Architecture" we are signifying our commitment to a CoP-informed pedagogy and practice: we are working on the basis that this Learning Architecture will provide the foundations from which a CoP will grow. This requires a commitment to a particular perspective on learning (that it is situated, that it is a social practice, that it is emergent), on patterns of participation (learners can follow different trajectories), on engagement (the importance of providing opportunities for authentic participation and reification), and so forth. If we agree that CoP theory best explains our work as university teachers and how we work with our students, then our CoP-informed teaching begins with our curriculum planning and designing – our Learning Architectures.

References

Brosnan, K., & Burgess, R. (2003). Web based continuing professional development – A learning architecture approach. *Journal of Workplace Learning*, 15(1), 24–33.

Case, J. (2015). Emergent interactions: Rethinking the relationship between teaching and learning. *Teaching in Higher Education*, 20(6), 625–635.

Chaiklin, S., & Lave, J. (Eds.). (1996). *Understanding practice: Perspectives on activity and context*. Cambridge University Press.

Cousin, G., & Deepwell, F. (2005). Designs for network learning: A communities of practice perspective. *Studies in Higher Education*, 30(1), 57–66.

Creanor, L., & Walker, S. (2005). Learning architectures and negotiation of meaning in European trade unions. *ALT-J*, 13(2), 109–123.

Jarvis, P. (Ed.). (2006). *The theory and practice of teaching* (2nd ed.). Routledge.

Jawitz, J. (2007). New academics negotiating communities of practice: Learning to swim with the big fish. *Teaching in Higher Education*, 12(2), 185–197.

Kirshner, D., & Whitson, J. (Eds.). (1997). *Situated cognition: Social, semiotic and psychological perspectives*. Lawrence Erlbaum Associates.

Lave, J., & Wenger, E. (1991). *Situated learning: Legitimate peripheral participation*. Cambridge University Press.

Lemke, J. (1997). Cognition, context and learning: A social semiotic perspective. In D. Kirshner, & J. Whitson (Eds.), *Situated cognition: Social, semiotic and psychological perspectives* (pp. 37–56). Lawrence Erlbaum.

McLoughlin, M., Lee, M., & Brady, J. (2008). A learning architecture framework (LAF) for developing community, engagement and professional identity for pre-service teachers. In I. Olney, G. Lefoe, J. Mantei, & J. Herrington (Eds.), *Proceedings of the second emerging technologies conference 2008* (pp. 147–157). University of Wollongong.

Scanlan, M. (2012). A learning architecture: How school leaders can design for learning social justice. *Educational Administration Quarterly, 49*(2), 348–391.

Smith, A. (2009). A case study of learning architecture and reciprocity. *International Journal of Early Childhood, 41*(1), 33–49.

Sorensen, E., & Ó Murchú, D. (2004). Designing online learning communities of practice: A democratic perspective. *Journal of Educational Media, 29*(3), 189–200.

Tight, M. (2018). *Higher education research: The developing field.* Bloomsbury.

Wenger, E. (1998). *Communities of practice: Learning, meaning and identity.* Cambridge University Press.

Wenger, E. (2000). Communities of practice and social learning systems. *Organisation, 7*(2), 225–246.

Wenger, E., McDermott, R., & Snyder, W. (2002). *Cultivating communities of practice.* Harvard Business School Press.

Wertsch, J., Del Río, P., & Alvarez, A. (Eds.). (1995). *Sociocultural studies of mind.* Cambridge University Press.

Chapter 5

Communities of Practice
Expansions and Limitations

Introduction

In this chapter, I introduce some of the more commonly found critiques of Communities of Practice (CoPs) theory and discuss the ways in which these have been addressed by different researchers and writers. CoP theory has been augmented in various ways over time, sometimes informed by empirical research that has in turn put the theory under strain and demanded new explanations for observed phenomena, and at other times informed by conceptual or philosophical critiques that have led to the resolution of these critiques through employing insights from other disciplinary bodies of knowledge. Having already noted the elasticity inherent in CoP theory in Chapter 2, we can now test that elasticity further by plugging in new perspectives and insights from different, though in some ways related, bodies of empirical and theoretical work.

Theory Building and Communities of Practice

The work of Jay Lemke (1997), as discussed in Chapter 4, provides a first example of a development or augmentation of CoP theory. As the theory has become established and evolved, it has come under increased scrutiny as researchers from a variety of disciplinary backgrounds – linguistics and sociolinguistics, management studies, philosophy, and education studies – have identified and then provided solutions to perceived conceptual difficulties or ambiguities (Tight, 2015; Tummons, 2014). Sometimes this is done through a reconsideration of the conceptual materials that Lave and Wenger have left us with, informed by additional empirical work. Lemke's conceptual addition is one example; another comes in the work of Harris and Shelswell (2005), who in their empirical study of an adult education programme proposed the concept of *Illegitimate* Peripheral Participation. In the original work, Lave and Wenger suggested that "there may very well be no such thing as an "illegitimate peripheral participant". The form that the legitimacy of participation takes is [...] a crucial condition for learning" (Lave & Wenger, 1991, p. 35). Harris and

Shelswell (2005) argued quite the opposite, however. In their research, they described how, over time, a minority of the members of this adult education CoP would try to shape or influence how the CoP would work or to dominate group discourse within the CoP, by drawing on previous experiences or skills that were significant aspects of the participant's identity in the past but which were outside the practice of the current CoP. On such occasions, when this minority would attempt to force such elements of their identity and past practice into the CoP – often causing friction and/or resistance from the other members – a form of disruption or conflict emerged. For Harris and Shelswell, this was a form of peripheral participation that fell outside the joint enterprise of the CoP, and therefore it was illegitimate (Harris & Shelswell, 2005, p. 168).

A more commonly found approach is the use of additional theoretical frameworks and concepts. Borrowing Bruno Latour's (2005) metaphor, I refer to these as theoretical *plug-ins* (Tummons, 2018). In computing, a plug-in is a piece of software that adds a new feature to an existing computer application. Here, we can use "plug-in" to refer to a new theoretical element that allows our main theory to do some new things that otherwise it would not be able to do. Just as with the computer software, though, our theoretical plug-in needs to be *compatible* with our main theory. Sometimes plug-ins are poorly chosen or misapplied, and this leads to theoretical incompatibilities.

One of the ways in which education researchers engage in theory building is through drawing on two – sometimes more – theories at the same time in order to see how they might complement each other and in turn shed new light on the problem being explored. CoP theory has been augmented, variously, by recourse to Bernsteinian curriculum theory, activity theory, actor-network theory, and both Foucauldian and Bourdieuian sociologies. These combinations work because even though the two parts of each combination are of course different, they are nonetheless compatible because they share some common ground in terms of their intellectual foundations. When we are theory building by combining different theoretical perspectives, therefore, we need to ensure that our two components are compatible with each other. They need to have epistemological and ontological compatibility if they are going to be able to work together, in just the same way that a freshly downloaded app needs to be compatible with the operating system of your laptop or phone: if you are running an incompatible operating system, then the app won't work.

Summing Up: Communities of Practice and Learning Architectures

Up to this point, we have established that:

1 A CoP is a shared space – physical and/or online and/or blended – in which people have come together in order to take part in a shared form of practice.

2. Practices are many and varied: some are time-consuming and complex, and others are more straightforward. Some involve complicated equipment and esoteric bodies of knowledge. They often require specialist ways of talking and/or writing.
3. Levels of participation are likewise variable: some people will travel towards the centre of the community, whilst others will always only stay nearer the boundaries. Some will change their direction of travel. Some will leave after a short time. Some will be asked to leave or even required to do so.
4. Membership of any CoP always involves learning, which is understood as a social practice. Learning is a necessary consequence of participation within the community.
5. Particular opportunities for new members of the community always need to be made available if they are going to be able to take part and hence to learn through Legitimate Peripheral Participation.
6. CoPs are everywhere and evolve over time. They always change – sometimes quickly and sometimes slowly. Sometimes they fade away. At other times, they change quite radically.
7. CoPs do not exist in isolation: they are always part of a wider constellation of CoPs, sometimes close together and sometimes at a distance. Borders overlap, people visit other CoPs and can be members of many, and objects, routines, ways of talking, and artefacts from one CoP can be borrowed – or stolen – by another. This is discussed in more depth in Chapter 6.
8. A CoP cannot be established in a top-down manner. But what we can do is design a Learning Architecture from which a CoP will develop. This allows us to place CoPs within formal educational structures/contexts. In making this statement, I adhere to the academic rather than practitioner model of CoPs.
9. Learning (according to our social theory) is emergent – it doesn't travel in a straight line. Therefore, the nature of CoPs is also emergent.
10. There are many social configurations of people and things that are of great interest to us as education researchers, but these are not necessarily CoPs. If we want to establish whether something is a CoP or not, then we have to do some research.

One of the critiques that has been levelled at the broader CoP literature (not without some justification) is that it tends to portray CoPs as being generally benign and friendly places, with disagreements restricted to generally polite conversations about the academic or professional matters at hand. Yes, there are possibilities for conflict – but these are framed in terms of intergenerational disagreements over practices or ideas, where the conflict is between new and old practices, habits, and repertoires rather than between new and old community members. Some of the more critical voices in the literature have argued that CoP theory lacks a way of accounting for conflict between members, cannot explain inequalities of power, and lacks tools and vocabulary for dealing with diversity and stigma. Others have suggested that CoP theory cannot accommodate wider societal issues, or account for the broader social and historical contexts in which CoPs find themselves. They look outward to other CoPs and other constellations, but they do not look at the rest of the world. For some writers, many of these concerns are due to flaws in CoP theory itself are perhaps generated as a result of incomplete or vague theorising, or possibly are due to a failure to consider certain key issues in the first place. These writers have resolved these deficiencies through recourse to other theoretical frameworks and perspectives.

It seems to me that there are five apposite areas for discussion within CoP theory. These are discussions that have foregrounded a number of aspects of the theory that are perhaps only briefly or vaguely articulated or otherwise rendered problematic, perhaps due to a lack of clarity or a detailed explanation. They are: how people talk in CoPs; gender; the position of the agentic individual within CoPs; the ethics of identity formation; and – perhaps the most frequently commented on – power and influence. These will be discussed in turn.

How People Talk in Communities of Practice

The work of Karin Tusting, and specifically her exploration of Wenger's concept of negotiation of meaning (Tusting, 2005; Wenger, 1998, p. 52), provides a good example of how to augment CoP theory so as to resolve a perceived structural weakness. In order to make meaning within a CoP, to begin to not only learn but also understand things, Wenger proposes that a two-way process called a *negotiation* is at work between our practice – our actions, behaviours, and speech – within a CoP on the one hand, and the ways in which the stuff of the CoP – the tools, routines, materials, and habits – are invented, used, or adapted. For Tusting, this is an element of CoP theory that requires more explanation (Tusting, 2005). Her approach leads her – and us – to think more deeply about the role of language within this negotiation of meaning. She suggests that if we really want to know more about the negotiation of meaning within a CoP, we need to use a more sophisticated theoretical approach to language than the one used by Wenger. Specifically, Tusting proposes using approaches derived from *linguistics* – the systematic study of human language which, when blended with CoP theory, helps us to make sense of language in relation to all of the other social practices at work within any CoP. In this way, we can explore how language is used to express personal identities or describe social structures, and how different genres of text carry different meanings for different members of the CoP.

Tusting's argument is that there is a relative lack of conceptual tools within CoP theory to make sense of how people talk and how they write, and of how different kinds of language use can have different consequences or implications.

The importance of discourse – written and spoken – is evident within CoP theory but lacks specificity. For example, we know that discourses are important not only within individual CoPs but across constellations and that they can help people coordinate practice or convince and persuade others about the merits or otherwise of differing perspectives. Discourses are not practices, however, but aspects of shared repertoire – material resources that can be used in a variety of contexts (Wenger, 1998, p. 129). But any definition of discourse is taken for granted within CoP theory, glossed over relatively swiftly. Within CoP theory, discourse is the resource that members use to describe and make sense of not only the practice of the community but the entire world (Wenger, 1998, p. 83). Language and literacy are self-evidently important, as the different vignettes from Wenger's own empirical research demonstrate. But *how* do they do what they do? To answer this, Tusting proposes that researchers pay closer attention to language use through discourse analysis.

For example, if we listen in to people talking within a CoP, are we listening to an argument about something, an explanation of something, or a description of something? An argument might be an indicator of inter-generational disagreement – a clash between a newcomer and an old-timer within the CoP. This might be focused on process or procedure, or perhaps, it might involve disagreement over an element of practice or an aspect of knowing. An explanation might be an indicator of a process of acculturation, of an old-timer instructing a newcomer into some aspect of the community's practice or history. But it might equally be a series of instructions simply to copy or repeat a procedure, without any understanding or evaluation. A description might be a rich account of a specific tool or artefact, explaining not only how it is used but also how it evolved from an earlier prototype to the more "polished" item being discussed. But it might also be a simplistic, reductive label that provides only a superficial description. All these are phenomena within CoPs that Wenger describes, anticipates, and theorises. All that is lacking is a clear explanation as to *how* we might come to identify and understand them. We might anticipate that an ethnographic approach would be appropriate here – after all, both of our seminal texts (*Situated Learning* and *Communities of Practice*) rest on ethnographies – but we also need something to provide a more fine-grained analysis. And this is what Tusting proposes. More recently, the related discipline of *sociolinguistics* – the study of societal effects on language and language use – has also begun to draw on CoP theory and to link it to the concept of the *speech community* which is prevalent in sociolinguistics (Meyerhoff & Strycharz, 2013).

Gender and Communities of Practice

Gender theory explores what is feminine and/or masculine – or neither, or both – across a range of social contexts and behaviour, and the objects or phenomena that come under scrutiny from this standpoint might range from educational curricula to the experiences of people at work. This way of understanding gender can be traced back to at least the end of the nineteenth century (Ritzer & Stepnisky, 2018). Gender is relatively unexplored from a CoP perspective (Brannan, 2007), but a small number of important contributions can be identified. Carrie Paechter has asked the question: what if masculinities or femininities are CoPs? She pluralises these in order to reflect that being feminine and/or masculine, or neither, can take different forms depending on cultural context, geography, age, and so forth (Paechter, 2003). If part of what being feminine or being masculine is relies on learning about them in a social context, then perhaps CoP theory can provide an additional tool for inquiry? Paechter illustrates her argument through using several key elements of CoP theory. For example, if we accept that being feminine or being masculine is changeable according to social or cultural contexts – that there are different "kinds" of both and these change over time and across social spaces – then we can think about the *boundaries* that might wrap around femininity or masculinity as a CoP. Similarly, Wenger's ideas about *identity* – which is part of the process of learning through Legitimate Peripheral Participation – are discussed in terms of practice: for example, certain forms of masculinity are formed through practices related to competitive sports, and this allows young men to both form their own identities and also project or display that identity to others within the community (Paechter, 2003, p. 74).

Paechter's approach allows us to draw on post-structuralist accounts of the social construction and performance of gender and reconcile this to a CoP perspective. This is a well-established field of study, and there are any number of possible areas for inquiry within higher education that can be explored through a gender lens, ranging from academic promotion to staff evaluations (Aiston & Fo, 2020; Heffernan, 2023) and from pedagogy to curriculum (Bagilhole & Goode, 1998; Hinton-Smith et al., 2021). The idea that different sociocultural phenomena can be differently gendered is well-established within education research. CoP theory, in and of itself, does not have any tools with which to tackle this issue (Hughes et al., 2007). Paechter's work provides a conduit for aligning gender theory with CoP theory.

Paechter draws on the academic model of CoPs, providing an expansive lens for inquiry that might allow us to think about masculinities and femininities as heuristic devices within a social practice context. A very different approach is taken by Thomson et al. (2022) in their account of a multinational and cross-institutional project funded by the European Union as part of the Horizon 2020 programme. The ACT-On-Gender project set out to find ways in which CoPs – here understood from the perspective of the practitioner model – could be used as vehicles for gender equity work in the HE sector. With a focus on seven identified CoPs that were variously boundaried in terms of geography, subject disincline, and institutions, Thomson and colleagues found that a CoP approach generated multiple ways of knowing and sharing expertise and practice that could in turn inform gender equity work. This CoP approach helped project participants think about a number of issues, such as the ways in which diversity of opinion within institutions might be managed or the reason why gender equity work was not always perceived as "real work" within academic contexts and therefore not evaluated for the purposes of promotion or progression. A further finding from the project was the extent to which individual activism and agency were leveraged by project participants when engaged in gender equity work, due to the lack of support from the institution and/or senior leadership – for example, in not having sufficient workload time or budgetary allocations to help support gender equity work. This is a phenomenon which is not unfamiliar to many of us in higher education and, as such, constitutes an important empirical finding. But there is also an important theoretical finding present – which, entirely understandably, Thomson and colleagues do not foreground in their conclusions – and which relates to the notion of individual agency within any CoP.

The Agentic Individual and Communities of Practice

Stephen Billett has written extensively about learning in a variety of workplace contexts. He has also drawn on this wider empirical work to critique elements of CoP theory, specifically, the ways in which the individual person is often lost sight of within the CoP literature. His concern is that within the social turn – the shift away from individual psychological models of cognition in favour of sociocultural accounts such as those espoused by Lave and Wenger – "the particular attributes that individuals bring to cognitive processes (i.e., the person and the personal) have become de-emphasized and in some cases overlooked" (Billett, 2007, p. 55). The concern is that "humans are subject to emotion, inconsistency in responses, exhaustion and inept responses *that are not adequately accounted for in either cognitive or social constructivist accounts*" (Billett, 2007, p. 56, emphasis added). Here, the argument is – simply put – that the socioculturalists have thrown out the baby with the bathwater. By focusing so closely – one might even say relentlessly – on the social and the distributed (in terms of practice, of learning, of cognition, and of knowledge), the contribution of the individual – shaped by disposition, family, life history, or the simple fact of getting older and acquiring experience – has been overlooked. Drawing on his own empirical work, Billett overcomes these difficulties through proposing the notion of *co-participation* as a way of foregrounding the two-way relationship between the social (that is, the CoP) and the individual (that is, the member, irrespective of trajectory). Where is the person, the individual, in the CoP? At different times, Wenger discusses ideas about identity, memory, how adults can be role models, and even histories of learning. But these topics are always, entirely understandably, brought back to the CoP as the focus for analysis. Identity is a consequence of participation in the community; memory is discussed only in contrast to the physical artefacts such as documents that are always and necessarily found within CoPs; the potential for adults to serve as role models is restricted to old-timers as representatives of specific CoPs; and histories of learning are discussed in terms of practice within the life-cycle of the CoP.

Here we can discern a further example of the shift in emphasis in CoP theory over time. In the earlier book, Lave and Wenger suggest a theory of practice – that is to say, of learning – that of necessity has to be situated within the historical development of the ongoing actions of society more generally and within CoPs more specifically (although it is important to remember that these remain only loosely defined). But they also take account of the capability and capacity for individuals to take decisions, of individual agency. "Participation, at the core of our theory of learning, *can be neither fully internalized […] nor fully externalized*" (Lave & Wenger, 1991, p. 51, emphasis added). From a situated perspective, they are not losing sight of the individual but instead they are proposing a new point of view: "participation in social practice – subjective as well as objective – *suggests a very explicit focus on the person*, but as person-in-the-world, as member of a sociocultural community" (Lave & Wenger, 1991, p. 52, emphasis added). This idea that we need not only the community but also the person, the one relying on and supporting the other, is an example of a *relational* perspective – an idea found more widely in social research generally. In order to make sense of the community we need to understand the place of the individual within it – and *vice versa*. Lave and Wenger certainly wanted the focus to shift away from being solely on the individual, but they never meant for the individual to be subsumed entirely by the CoP. However, in a manner similar to other elements of their work, this relational perspective has been lost sight of. The work of Billett helps to correct this.

Concepts of individual autonomies and freedoms, or *agencies*, within different kinds of social environments have been explored in depth by a number of sociological researchers. A discussion of *agency* could fill a much larger book than this one, so here I will refer to the definition provided by the sociologist Anthony Giddens: "agency concerns events of which an individual is a perpetrator […] whatever happened would not have happened if that individual had not intervened" (Giddens, 1984, p. 9). There are other definitions and other writers who would disagree with Giddens. It remains the case that agency is under-explored within CoP theory, and ideas about agency from wider sociological research do provide a useful way to think about this.

The Ethics of Identity Formation in Communities of Practice

A similarly sharpened focus on the individual within the CoP underpins the work of Sarid and Levanon (2022) who, in common with several other authors, foreground the ways in which CoP theory overlooks particular aspects of the educational process (and it is noteworthy that their discussion is framed in terms of education, which implies a formal structure and formal pedagogical relationships, rather than in terms of learning or practice more generally). The kernel of their argument is that Wenger "disregards the role of ethics or moral values in the process of personal development" (Sarid & Levanon, 2022, p. 1697) but that through the inclusion of additional theoretical components – referred to as supplementation – these *lacunae* can be resolved. There are two aspects to this. The first and most straightforward is a call to encourage critical reflection as posited by Jack Mezirow as an essential aspect of the transformative learning of adults. For Mezirow, learning entails, amongst other things, an increasing capacity to analysing things in a manner increasingly removed from personal or local perspectives. This capacity is engendered through the *critical reflection on assumptions.* This process of critical self-reflection in turn allows the individual community member to develop an "ethical imagination" (Sarid & Levanon, 2022, p. 1700). Drawing on the work of the philosopher Charles Taylor, Sarid and Levanon propose that identity formation within CoPs requires the establishment of a relationship between an individual and the contextual framework of meaning (the CoP) from which the individual can draw. This process of identity formation is, therefore, a further example of negotiation between the individual and the community (Wenger, 1998, p. 210): the individual negotiates their identity in relation to the practice of the community – what is significant, what is known and talked about, how things are done, and so forth. In drawing on Taylor, Sarid and Levanon bring an ethical dimension into play: the negotiation of identity necessarily involves making *strong evaluations* that require the individual to consider their own values and motivations.

This ethical shift in identity formation has consequences for the individual not only as they reflect critically on their values both within and without the context for meaning-making generated by the CoP, but also as they negotiate their identity and place in relation to other members of the CoP. For example, negotiations between novices and experts concerning matters to do with the practices of the community – how a routine ought to be performed, how an artefact ought to be employed, whether or not an innovation should be adopted – tend to be framed in the context of the practice itself. The expert gains a degree of authority from the very fact of having expertise – an authority that the novice cannot access but only aspire to in the future. The negotiations of meaning that take place between any novice and any expert are therefore concentrated on knowing and knowledgeability – conversations, decisions, exchanges, and so forth that are strongly framed by the ways of knowing of the CoP. But thanks to Sarid and Levanon, we can now also frame these negotiations in terms of an ethics that may conflict with local – that is, indigenous to the community – ways of knowing and meaning (Sarid & Levanon, 2022, p. 1701). This has implications for how the relationships between novices and experts are made sense of. Yes, the differences between them continue to rest on knowledge and expertise (arguably as forms of capital), but they also now rest on a more or less universal ethics that necessarily speaks to concerns that transcend the particular CoP within which the expert and the novice find themselves and that consequently shifts the hierarchical relationship between them. Simply put, the ethical shift adds to how we might make sense of power relationships or power imbalances within CoPs. This is an important contribution because the ways in which matters of power within CoPs are theorised have long been a focus for criticism.

Power and Influence Within Communities of Practice

The criticism that CoP theory lacks appropriate conceptual tools for the explanation or analysis of power (which might include control, conflict, stigma, and so forth) and subsequently of resistance (refusal, disagreement, strategic compliance, and so forth) is well-established (Barton & Hamilton, 2005; Boylan, 2010). The lack of such tools raises difficult questions. How should we make sense of inter-generational conflicts between newcomers who are seeking to adjust the practices of the community or introduce new innovations, and those old-timers who are resistant to change of any kind? What if apprentices are deliberately blocked from the legitimate peripheral practices of the community – how will they then learn? What if old-timers are prevented from accessing new elements of the shared repertoire? Who monitors the boundaries of a CoP? Who or what is allowed in, and who or what is excluded, and on what grounds? Accounting for power within CoPs requires further theoretical augmentation. Here are two examples.

Fox (2000), in his account of power relations within CoPs, highlights a further example of the distance between Lave and Wenger (1991) and Wenger (1998): in the earlier work, useful – if once again all-too-brief – concepts for thinking about inequalities of influence and power within a CoP are provided in the two contradictions of contradiction and change, and continuity and displacement. But these are lost sight of in the later work. The continuity/displacement contradiction is worth discussing in a little more detail, as it opens up possibilities for inquiry such as conflict, changing power relations between subsequent generations of CoP members, and even the notion of "submissive imitation" (Lave & Wenger, 1991, p. 116). In order to reintroduce these into the academic CoP model of the later book, Fox draws on the work of Michel Foucault. He proposes that Foucault's idea of power as being constantly created and recreated through unequal relations straightforwardly plugs into CoP theory: the greater time served within the CoP that is enjoyed by the experienced older participant provides a *de facto* inequality in relation to the inexperienced newcomer that therefore generates a power imbalance between the two participants. But this will not necessarily lead to conflict: whether or not such a power imbalance has negative or harmful consequences (as it were) will always depend on context – on the nature of the CoP in question, on the identities of the participants, and so forth. How power works within a CoP needs to be explained every time, therefore, and not taken for granted or presented in a normative fashion.

Davies (2005), drawing on sociolinguistics, also problematises some of the core elements of CoP theory in her explication of power and influence within CoPs. Firstly, in unpacking notions of membership of CoPs, she interrogates the distinction between peripherality and marginality. The former indicates that the member in question will be allowed to follow a trajectory that will lead to fuller participation over time; the latter indicates a more or less permanent position at the fringes of the CoP. Simply put, some are allowed to proceed while others are marginalised. Davies concludes that "it must be a question of *sanction*" (Davies, 2005, p. 566) – but who decides? At the same time, she demonstrates how membership – of any nature – relies on not only access to practice but *acceptance* into the practice. Such a process of acceptance implies the presence of mechanisms for gate-keeping within the CoP (as distinct from the gate-keeping employed to patrol/protect the boundaries of a CoP – I shall return to this in Chapter 6). These mechanisms must be employed by some people either in or against the interests of others, thereby in turn implying a hierarchical power structure within the CoP. Davies concludes that CoP theory needs to be further developed through empirical research in order to account for hierarchies such as these.

These and other accounts have set out to resolve the problem of power within CoPs, with varying degrees of success. At the same time, it is worth noting that Wenger himself has responded unequivocally to this longstanding critique of CoP theory: "it is a learning theory, not a theory of power in general [...] if you want to look at the broader political context in which the local definition of competence is taking place, there are plenty of existing theories that address power at that level. So there is no need to reinvent them" (Farnsworth et al., 2016, p. 153).

Summing Up: Resolving Conceptual Problems in Communities of Practice Theory

Over time, several deficiencies in CoP theory have been identified. Some of these have been frequently noted (e.g., the lack of theoretical tools to account for power and influence), whilst others occupy a more niche position (e.g., the interpolation of an ethics of identity formation). However they are resolved, these critiques:

- Are derived from empirical and/or theoretical/philosophical inquiries.
- Demonstrate how epistemologically and ontologically related perspectives can be used to augment CoP theory.
- Illustrate the ongoing utility of CoP theory as an explanatory framework with the capacity to consider matters not anticipated or described in depth by Lave and Wenger.

Dysfunction Within Communities of Practice

Disagreements between experts and novices, old-timers and newcomers, within CoPs provide just one example of how relations within CoPs can break down. CoPs are not *a priori* harmonious structures, of course, and the necessary presence of tensions, even conflicts, within CoPs is acknowledged by Wenger (1998). But this need not lead automatically to a breakdown of practice. So long as mutual engagement, joint enterprise, and shared repertoire are *sufficiently* maintained, the CoP can continue to work. Relations within communities will not always be harmonious; they simply need to be harmonious enough.

In the move from the academic model to the practitioner model (Wenger et al., 2002), rather different kinds of possible breakdowns emerge. With the focus moving from a bottom-up, "organic" perspective on CoPs to a top-down, "structural" perspective, it is the CoP, rather than the people within the CoP, which becomes the object of inquiry. Some of these possible breakdowns or downsides clearly reflect the managerial/organisational focus of the practitioner model: for example, the concern that CoPs may be willing to accept mediocrity on the grounds that "it is sometimes easier to … settle for less than cutting-edge" (Wenger et al., 2002, p. 149) may well align neatly to the corporate knowledge-management strategies that the practitioner model speaks to, but seems out of kilter with the anthropologically grounded CoPs described in the earlier works. Other possible causes of breakdown or dysfunction within the practitioner model are backwardly compatible with, and demonstrate traces of, the academic model, and are of particular relevance to universities, and these are worth considering in a little more detail.

- Documentism and amnesia

    The bureaucratisation of higher education and the accompanying growth of audit cultures have long been subjects for academic inquiry (Murphy, 2009; Shore & Wright, 1999, 2000). And as we have already established, any CoP – whether disciplinary, inter-disciplinary or departmental – both constructs and uses a wide variety of artefacts or reifications, consequent to and necessary for participation in practice. Documentism describes the phenomenon of excessive documentation, of the proliferation of forms, papers, PDF files, templates, reports, and so forth that lubricate the processes of higher education institutions but also slow them down. It is beyond the scope of this book to evaluate those critiques of contemporary higher education that identify bureaucratisation and audit culture as generating more or less unforeseen degradations in academic work. Nonetheless, it is perhaps not too fanciful to suggest that for some readers of this book, the proliferation of paperwork in higher education – documentism – can be recognised as problematic. The opposite of documentism is amnesia, and this is described by Wenger. McDermott and Snyder quite simply as the lack of a sufficient documentary history of process and practice within a CoP. Ideally, a balance needs to be struck between these two extremes.

- Exclusivity

    In the following chapter, we shall explore the extent to which different CoPs work together, share resources, materials and people, and build relationships across boundaries. One key consequence of this network of connections is that no CoP is entirely isolated from any other. Ways of doing and knowing are in constant circulation to varying degrees, and practices and shared and borrowed. But what happens when a CoP exerts such a strong hold on the domain of practice that it becomes exclusive? For Wenger, McDermott and Snyder, the consequences are unambiguous: "… outsiders are likely to feel hostage to the self-righteous expertise of specialists" (Wenger et al., 2002, p. 142). There is no reason to assume that universities would not behave like any other workplace and be prone from time to time to factionalism, the emergence of cliques, disconnectedness between individuals and/or departments, and so forth (Oliver & Morris, 2022). Whilst we might question the extent to which exclusivity rests on "self-righteous" expertise, we can nonetheless recognise the tensions that arise when faced with sets of practices, discourses or ways of knowing – these might pertain equally to research methodologies and epistemological standpoints, or to procedural or organisational processes – that have been "black-boxed" and brook no discussion or disagreement.

- Dogmatism

    Notwithstanding the inherent changeability of CoPs, members can nonetheless be more or less rigid in their negotiation of practice and resist attempts to introduce variation, let alone novelty. Commitment to the joint enterprise of the CoP, to the appropriate use of the shared repertoire, and to the established processes for mutual engagement needs to be reflexive, not unyielding. Particularly when faced with an impetus for change from outside the CoP, members can be needlessly resistant, perhaps using their own esoteric ways of knowing and specialised discourse as a barrier to negotiation. Recent histories of educational technology uptake in higher education provide a clear example of such dogmatism, in this instance in relation to the competing interests, politics, and passions of technology evangelists on the one hand and technology sceptics on the other, on individual resistance to and strategic compliance with institution-wide policies, and on the unhelpful oversimplifications ("educational technology is always good and it is always what students want") used in such contexts (Blin & Munro, 2008; Habib & Johannesen, 2014; Liu et al., 2020). One of the core functions of any university is to embrace and expand on multiple ways of knowing, but this does not prevent the people within them from behaving like workers in any other organisation, capable of uncritical commitment to particular points of view or forms of practice.

Conclusion: Expansions and Limitations

Any theoretical framework has limits. CoP theory can be stretched and reshaped to some degree, but there are some places that it can't go without help. In this chapter, I have focused on some of the themes that have attracted critique from a number of researchers and writers. This is a critique that is not always fully justified (particularly when noting Wenger's own response to critiques of explanations of power within CoPs) but that nonetheless deserves a response. In doing so, I have drawn on prior research in order to give examples of different ways through which these critiques might be addressed. The researchers whom I have referred to in this chapter are not setting out to dismantle CoP theory, rather, they have drawn on other perspectives that are sympathetic to a CoP approach and that we can, therefore, use alongside CoP theory in order to unpack and understand those issues and problems that Lave and Wenger (1991) and Wenger (1998) cannot reach.

References

Aiston, S., & Fo, C. (2020). The silence/ing of academic women. *Gender and Education*, 33(2), 138–155.

Bagilhole, B., & Goode, J. (1998). The "Gender dimension" of both the "Narrow" and "Broad" curriculum in UK higher education: Do women lose out in both? *Gender and Education*, 10(4), 445–458.

Barton, D., & Hamilton, M. (2005). Literacy, reification and the dynamics of social interaction. In D. Barton, & K. Tusting (Eds.), *Beyond communities of practice: Language, power and social context* (pp. 14–35). Cambridge University Press.

Billett, S. (2007). Including the missing subject: Placing the personal within the community. In J. Hughes, N. Jewson, & L. Unwin (Eds.), *Communities of practice: Critical perspectives* (pp. 55–67). Routledge.

Blin, F., & Munro, M. (2008). Why Hasn't technology disrupted academics' teaching practices? Understanding resistance to change through the lens of activity theory. *Computers and Education*, 50(2), 475–90.

Boylan, M. (2010). Ecologies of participation in school classrooms. *Teaching and Teacher Education*, 26(1), 61–70.

Brannan, M. (2007). Sexuality, gender and legitimate peripheral participation: An ethnographic study of a call centre. In J. Hughes, N. Jewson, & L. Unwin (Eds.), *Communities of practice: Critical perspectives* (pp. 120–130). Routledge.

Davies, B. (2005). Communities of practice: Legitimacy not choice. *Journal of Sociolinguistics*, 9(4), 557–581.

Farnsworth, V., Kleanthous, I., & Wenger-Trayner, E. (2016). Communities of practice as A social theory of learning: A conversation with Etienne Wenger. *British Journal of Educational Studies*, 64(2), 139–160.

Fox, S. (2000). Communities of practice, Foucault and actor-network theory. *Journal of Management Studies*, 37(6), 853–867.

Giddens, A. (1984). *The constitution of society: Outline of the theory of structuration*. University of California Press.

Habib, L., & Johannesen, M. (2014). Perspectives on academic staff involvement in the acquisition and implementation of educational technologies. *Teaching in Higher Education*, 19(5), 484–496.

Harris, S., & Shelswell, N. (2005). Moving beyond communities of practice in adult basic education. In D. Barton, & K. Tusting (Eds.), *Beyond communities of practice: Language, power and social context* (pp. 158–179). Cambridge University Press.

Heffernan, T. (2023). Abusive comments in student evaluations of courses and teaching: The attacks women and marginalised academics endure. *Higher Education, 85*(1), 225–239.

Hinton-Smith, T., Marvell, R., Morris, C., & Brayson, K. (2021). 'It's not something that we think about with regard to curriculum.' Exploring gender and equality awareness in higher education curriculum and pedagogy. *Gender and Education, 34*(5), 495–511.

Hughes, J., Jewson, N., & Unwin, L. (Eds.). (2007). *Communities of practice: Critical perspectives*. Routledge.

Latour, B. (2005). *Reassembling the social: An introduction to actor-network theory*. Clarendon Press.

Lave, J., & Wenger, E. (1991). *Situated learning: Legitimate peripheral participation*. Cambridge University Press.

Lemke, J. (1997). Cognition, context and learning: A social semiotic perspective. In D. Kirshner, & J. Whitson (Eds.), *Situated cognition: Social, semiotic and psychological perspectives* (pp. 37–56). Lawrence Erlbaum.

Liu, Q., Geertshuis, S., & Grainger, R. (2020). Understanding academics' adoption of learning technologies: A systematic review. *Computers and Education, 151*, 1–19.

Meyerhoff, M., & Strycharz, A. (2013). Communities of practice. In J. Chambers, & N. Schilling (Eds.), *The handbook of language variation and change* (pp. 428–447). Wiley-Blackwell.

Murphy, M. (2009). Bureaucracy and its limits: Accountability and rationality in higher education. *British Journal of Sociology of Education, 30*(6), 683–695.

Oliver, C., & Morris, A. (2022). Resisting the "academic circle jerk": Precarity and friendship at academic conferences in UK higher education. *British Journal of Sociology of Education, 43*(4), 603–622.

Paechter, C. (2003). Masculinities and femininities as communities of practice. *Women's Studies International Forum, 26*(1), 69–77.

Ritzer, G., & Stepnisky, J. (2018). *Sociological theory* (10th ed.). Sage.

Sarid, A., & Levanon, M. (2022). Rethinking the theory of communities of practice in education: Critical reflection and ethical imagination. *Educational Philosophy and Theory, 54*(10), 1693–1704.

Shore, C., & Wright, S. (1999). Audit culture and anthropology: New-liberalism in British higher education. *Journal of the Royal Anthropological Institute, 5*(4), 557–575.

Shore, C., & Wright, S. (2000). Coercive accountability – The rise of audit culture in higher education. In M. Strathern (Ed.), *Audit cultures: Anthropological studies in accountability, ethics and the academy* (pp. 57–89). Routledge.

Thomson, A., Palmén, R., Reidl, S., Barnard, S., Beranek, S., Dainty, A. R. J., & Hassan, T. M. (2022). Fostering collaborative approaches to gender equality interventions in higher education and research: The case of transnational and multi-institutional communities of practice. *Journal of Gender Studies, 31*(1), 36–54.

Tight, M. (2015). Theory application in higher education research: The case of communities of practice. *European Journal of Higher Education, 5*(2), 111–126.

Tummons, J. (2014). Learning architectures and communities of practice in higher education. In J. Huisman, & M. Tight (Eds.), *Theory and method in higher education research II* (pp. 121–139). Emerald.

Tummons, J. (2018). *Learning architectures in higher education: Beyond communities of practice*. Bloomsbury.

Tusting, K. (2005). Language and power in communities of practice. In D. Barton, & K. Tusting (Eds.), *Beyond communities of practice: Language, power and social context* (pp. 36–54). Cambridge University Press.

Wenger, E. (1998). *Communities of practice: Learning, meaning and identity.* Cambridge University Press.

Wenger, E., McDermott, R., & Snyder, W. (2002). *Cultivating communities of practice.* Harvard Business School Press.

Chapter 6

Constellations, Brokers, and Boundaries
How Communities of Practice Learn from and Work with Each Other

Introduction

In this chapter, we move beyond the confines of an individual Community of Practice (CoP) in order to think about the ways in which CoPs can work together and share resources. In explaining how CoPs as defined sociocultural units of practice and meaning-making can talk to each other, we shall consider how the boundaries of the communities are constituted and then how they can be crossed over, how people can be members of several communities and also be visitors to others, what kinds of practices happen specifically at the boundaries of a community, and how multiple communities might be organised as some kind of whole. In so doing, we can demonstrate that a university can be understood as a constellation of CoPs – an arrangement of related though distinct communities working towards a related joint enterprise.

Becoming a Professional Youth Worker

During our explorations of trajectories for learning in CoPs in higher education in Chapter 2, we considered the example of a student who aspires to be a professional youth worker and therefore enrols on an appropriate university programme, a degree in Youth Work, in order to obtain a qualification that will carry with it the requisite licence to practice. Our student, having travelled across a series of different learning trajectories that will have taken them from entry onto the degree programme through to graduation via a series of core and optional modules (a typical design for many undergraduate curricula), will finish this stage of their journey when entering the profession. Taken as a whole, this journey – from first-year student to newly qualified youth worker, graduation certificate in hand – has required our student to negotiate membership of a number of different CoPs, all of which either overlap or otherwise share aspects of practice to different degrees. Whether or not we describe these CoPs as academic disciplines or academic departments (as discussed in Chapter 3), our student has negotiated successful passage across all of them.

DOI: 10.4324/9781003412106-6

How did the journey start? Perhaps through reading about the course on the university's website, perhaps through attending an open day, then receiving a conditional offer for a place on the course. With the required entry qualifications obtained, our student can begin their journey across the curriculum through the mutual engagement offered by seminars and lectures, acquiring an appropriate understanding of the shared repertoire of journal articles, module handbooks, and appropriate ways of writing (reifications) in portfolios and talking in class, all centred on the joint enterprise of the CoP – the practice of youth work. Whether the degree programme is framed as being just one CoP or several overlapping ones, we can see the identity of our students being negotiated as they follow their trajectories, perhaps changing how they speak and/or write about youth work, certainly introducing what are, for them, new ways of knowing about youth work. During their time at university, our student may have been part of other CoPs as well – perhaps related to extra-curricular activities such as volunteering or student politics. Perhaps they volunteered to be a student helper during an open day, offering in turn the same kind of advice and help that they had received in the past. Whatever the precise journey followed by our student, we can confidently state that they have journeyed through a series of CoPs, some overlapping, others separate but closely aligned.

And how does the journey end? When leaving the CoP (or CoPs) of the youth work programme, our student takes with them two related documents or, better, textual artefacts: a degree transcript (the document, usually electronic, that specifies the grades awarded for individual modules as well as the overall degree classification awarded), and a degree certificate (usually although by no means always collected at a graduation ceremony, a physical document that is invariably presented in an ornate form, with a crest of arms or similar at the top, and so forth). It is difficult for our student to quickly and conveniently summarise all of their learning and experiences through talk, but these two pieces of paper represent an extremely effective, and well-established, technology for capturing – reifying – a variety of complex practices and experiences in a form which is easily transportable and therefore easy to share with recruitment firms and interview panels when looking for a first job in youth work. The degree credentials help the student get "over the line" and into work in just the same manner as their A-level certificates helped them join the degree programme in the first place.

A student no longer, our new youth worker will have much to learn as they start their new career. Having qualified with a degree shows that they know enough to 'get started', but the complexities of authentic professional practice cannot all be anticipated by the authors of the recently completed undergraduate curriculum. Degree programmes such as these are closely tied to a specific profession and are invariably mapped onto a series of standards that have been established by the relevant professional association – also a CoP (Weller, 2017). The degree provides the student with a threshold level of competence and expertise, sufficient to allow entry to the workforce, but with the assumption that professional/occupational learning will continue – as a consequence of ongoing engagement in legitimate professional practice (Eraut, 1994).

The journey taken by our imaginary student might easily have traced a learning journey through a history degree or a degree in physics or civil engineering. These other journeys will involve engagement in or with other CoPs that we have not yet considered, perhaps through industrial placements, career events, or site visits. That is to say, whilst the majority of their journey will have been characterised by participation in – probably – several related CoPs, at other times more fleeting or marginal encounters with other CoPs will have taken place. Our exploration of the CoPs that constitute higher education needs to consider not only those that we – as academics, as administrators, and as students – are members of but also those that we only occasionally come into contact with, that we negotiate with, that we might visit and interact with in some way but never become members of.

CoP theory provides us with several different conceptual tools for making sense of these different events. We can explore how people enter and leave CoPs by thinking about *boundaries* and *boundary crossings*. Fleeting connections with other CoPs, irrespective of any ambitions for future membership and participation, are described as *boundary encounters*. Remembering how not only people but also things (such as degree certificates) can travel from one CoP to another, we can explore the work done by *boundary objects*. We can consider the impact on our youth work students of their multiple journeys through different CoPs – sometimes as a member of more than one at the same time – in terms of *multimembership*. We can trace the overlaps and connections between CoPs as *constellations*. We have already mentioned boundaries and constellations in passing, but now they need more extensive treatment. And in unpacking these key elements of CoP theory, we will need to introduce a small number of additional theoretical components as we go.

Boundaries

In Chapter 1, we explored mutual engagement, joint enterprise, and shared repertoire: the paradigmatic components of any CoP (Wenger, 1998). If in our (observational) research we can discern each of these three elements at work, we can be confident that we are observing a CoP rather than any other kind of social formation. Moreover, it is in how these three things are accomplished that we can begin to discern the boundaries of the community in question – the places and spaces where the identifiable practices of the community start and stop.

The boundary of any CoP can be formed in several ways, some more conspicuous than others. For example, if we have chosen to frame academic disciplines/departments as CoPs, then we might start with the building in which that department is housed, although this would not preclude members of the CoP from utilising other physical or virtual spaces as necessary in order to accomplish the joint enterprise of the community. The concentration of activity within the department related to the academic subject in question – captured in wall hangings, the PhD students' common room, display cases containing books written by members of staff, monitors advertising departmental seminars, and so forth – provides a series of observable practices that can help us identify the CoP. The boundary of a CoP is in part, sometimes, reified through physical structures but cannot straightforwardly be limited to them. Yes, a Building Surveying department can be seen as a CoP, but it is not simply the fact that you would have to pass through a specific set of double doors to get to it that makes it a community with a tightly framed boundary. It is the nature of the practices of the community that make it distinct. What people do, what tools and techniques they use, how they speak and write about what they do, even how they might dress, and so forth – these are the things that the rest of us can see and hear that set the Community of Building Surveying Practice apart from the other communities that make up the constellation of a faculty or even an entire university.

In some CoPs, therefore, it will be in the ways that people dress that membership can be most straightforwardly identified: staff and students in anthropology or chemistry will often wear lab coats, and nursing or physiotherapy students will often wear uniforms. There's no uniform for linguistics or multimedia journalism degree students, but there are specialist vocabularies ("lexis", "phonology", "page layout", and "photojournalism") that form part of the shared repertoires of these two CoPs that contribute to their distinctiveness – that help form a linguistic boundary (here, the concept from sociolinguistics of the *speech community* is helpful). In other CoPs, it may be the workbooks or resources (physical or virtual) that students and/or teachers work with that distinguish them as members, or it may be the online spaces that they utilise.

Some of the tools and equipment that might be found in a chemistry lab will be the same as or similar to those found in a biology lab, but it is in how they are used and talked about that the disciplinary differences will emerge. The differences between two CoPs based on other academic subjects, by contrast, might take a little longer to tease apart. At first look, a sociology seminar might not seem particularly different to a law seminar – especially if the seminars are being housed in centrally timetabled shared teaching accommodation rather than in rooms based within departments. But more fine-grained observations will over time highlight the differences between them – the materials that the students are reading on their laptops, the different specialist vocabulary that is used, the disciplinary-specific assessment guidance provided by the teachers, and so forth.

The boundaries of any CoP are both physical and non-physical; therefore, they can be based on geography or on language use, on writing style, or on dress. They might be easy to identify or difficult for the outsider to discern. They might be very tightly framed or relatively loosely framed (Boud & Middleton, 2003). But they do not imply or effect isolationism; however, they are constituted, boundaries are sites for both entry and exit. It is in the ways that people and things cross over them that we can see the boundaries at work.

Boundary Crossings

Boundary crossing entails one of two possible outcomes: either that somebody needs to pay a temporary visit to a CoP without any intention of membership (and I shall return to visitors below); or, the outcome that occupies much more of the theory, that somebody wishes to become a member of the community. In these cases, boundary crossing takes place irrespective of the trajectories (as discussed in Chapter 2) that the newcomers might find themselves on or aspire to in the future: the new member's imagined trajectory may not end up being the one followed. The trajectory that our newcomer will imagine themselves following relates to their aspirations – their reasons for joining. A newcomer to the Community of Sports Science Practice who aspires to working in a professional context, perhaps becoming a strength and conditioning coach, will look for a trajectory that will always be *peripheral* and *outbound*, undertaking membership of this community solely to enable access to a different one, in industry, in due course. This is a peripheral trajectory because the newcomer is not aspiring to full membership, only to a sufficient depth of membership so as to gain certification; and it is an outbound trajectory because the newcomer is coming into the community with a fixed exit point already in mind.

However, the newcomer who is travelling in the other direction, who is coming from the sports science profession and is seeking to change career, to undertake postgraduate study and become a university lecturer, will follow a different, *inbound* trajectory. For this new student and aspirant academic, the trajectory is defined in part by their identity as already shaped by their past membership(s) of professional CoPs and by their *reconciliation work* in learning to balance what they have learned from the profession (where local practices, shortcuts, and workarounds are common features of work of which line managers and supervisors may well be entirely unaware (Belfiore et al., 2004)) with the specifications of a university postgraduate curriculum that will require more precise and standardised ways of working (although if the newcomer has previously studied at university, some of these will be familiar).

Nobody is either entitled to or guaranteed membership of any CoP. Even the most weakly framed CoP (Boud & Middleton, 2003) asks something of its members as well as providing opportunities for participation in return. There is, simply put an unavoidable gate-keeping aspect to a CoP that can help or hinder boundary crossing and that speaks to the issues of tensions and power within CoPs discussed in Chapter 5. Border crossings can be facilitated in different ways, depending on the nature of the person or people who want to gain entry. An academic department, a tightly framed CoP with a very clear and coherent joint enterprise, will look for quite specific things from the newcomers. A straightforward example of this would be the entry requirements that are attached to university programmes although these might be enacted in very different ways – through A-levels, combinations of A-levels and T-levels, BTECs, perhaps framed as contextual offers, and so forth. With the correct entry qualifications, entry to the CoP can be assured. However, this entry process has to be negotiated through a specific series of exchanges, or *encounters*, at the boundary.

Boundary Encounters

Boundary encounters come in different forms and involve different members of the CoP. *Brokering* (Wenger, 1998, pp. 108–113) is a commonly found, albeit quite specific, aspect of work of any CoP. It refers to any of the work that is done by those members who are responsible for making connections between different CoPs. Brokering involves operating at the boundaries of CoPs, building connections between different CoPs in order to facilitate coordinated effort, introducing the practices of one CoP into the repertoire of another so as to enable a new form of learning, representing the practices of one CoP to the members of another, helping move objects or tools between communities, and so forth (Wenger, 1998, p. 109). The negotiation of access is another aspect of brokering work in Communities of Higher Education Practice, and this can happen in a number of ways. If we think back to the experiences of our imaginary youth work student, we might describe the people that they spoke to at the open day as *brokers* – representatives of the practice that the student is seeking to join. The members of staff involved in making admissions decisions are likewise brokers. Brokerage processes can be reified in fixed forms such as open days and admissions tariffs. Brokerage processes can also be utilised by existing members of the community. A university-based work placement coordinator is a further example of a broker, this time one who represents the interests of the university when visiting employers and preparing the ground for future students who will take up internships as part of their programme of study.

Brokers can also help people who wish to have a look around a CoP as a *visitor* rather than from any desire to engage in practice (Wenger, 1998, p. 112). Visiting a CoP is a specific kind of boundary encounter that might be one-off, discrete event or might be paCort of a longer-standing relationship between two or more CoPs that are either already part of a group of constellations where practice can be shared or where greater collaboration is the planned-for outcome of the visit. For example, an academic might visit a research institute at another university with the aspiration or intention to generate a collaborative funding bid. Another academic might be asked to act as an external examiner, either for a degree programme or for a doctoral student's viva. Encounters such as these have the potential to lead to meaningful collaboration between different CoPs (designing new research ideas and evaluating a series of modules), to generate new forms of participation (research conversations, vivas, and conferences) and reification (funding bids, journal articles, and published curricula), and to encourage the sharing of people and things between the CoPs in question (sharing open-access datasets and research staff with split contracts).

Boundary Objects

Any object or artefact that reifies some aspect of shared repertoire – a tool, a routine, a document, a procedure – can be transported across the boundaries between two or more CoPs in a manner analogous to the ways in which people do. As we discussed in Chapter 4, CoPs are simultaneously global and local to differing degrees and regularly adopt, customise, or even steal elements of practice from other, more or less distant, communities with which they have some kind of brokering relationship. A tool might be borrowed or copied, then adapted, until after a certain period of time, the fact that the tool originally came from elsewhere is lost sight of although sometimes the history of an artefact can be more or less easily unearthed (e.g., a student in health professions asking why a catheter is called a *Foley* catheter and being told about the inventor, Dr Frederic Foley). For CoPs that are arranged in a constellation (discussed below), such commonalities of practice – overlaps and complementarities in shared repertoire, mutual engagement, or joint enterprise – are quite common.

But there are other kinds of tools and artefacts which also help to build connections between different communities but which, when dispatched from their "home" CoPs, do not become absorbed into or get co-opted by their "destination" CoPs. To describe these, Wenger draws on the work of Susan Leigh Star, a sociologist of science and technology, and specifically on her concept of the *boundary object* (Star & Griesemer, 1989; Wenger, 1998, pp. 106–108). Following Star, we can identify four types of boundary objects (although this was never intended to be a definitive taxonomy), and these are defined as follows (Star & Griesemer, 1989, pp. 410–411):

1 *Repositories.* A repository is something like a library or a museum. They consist simply of piles of objects (of whatever kind the repository is about) that have been grouped together using some kind of organising or indexing system to help people find the things that they need. These are easily recognisable within universities!
2 *Ideal types.* An ideal type (where ideal means "most suitable" rather than "perfect") is any object that is not an accurate representation of one specific thing but instead is a generalised abstraction – perhaps a diagram or a map. An ideal type is vague and lacking in specificity, but can be adopted to a

specific context relatively easily. A reflective practice writing frame for social work or teacher education students is an example of an ideal type.
3 *Coincident boundaries*. Objects that have coincident boundaries have the same boundaries as each other but different contents. A good example is found in the process of mapping: the same area might be mapped in two different ways by two different people, depending on what the mapping process sought to illustrate (e.g., a geological map as opposed to a topographical map, or a map of the human form that illustrates the nervous system as opposed to one that illustrates the lymphatic system). The same object is being described (a specified area of land and the human body), but different aspects of each are foregrounded.
4 *Standardised forms*. A standardised form is an object that has been constructed in such a way as to allow for communication across separate communities. Once the form has been designed, information will always be organised on the form in a consistent way, and this helps the form to travel between different locations, carrying with it the information in question. An example is given below.

Boundary objects, once incorporated into CoP theory, are defined as any kind of artefact that might help different stuff travel between different CoPs: materials, routines, forms of expression, messages, bodies of knowledge, codified information, and so on. Their defining characteristic, irrespective of type, is that they do not settle – either temporarily or permanently – into the CoP to which they have travelled. Their job is as a transmitter or conveyor of whatever it is that is being transmitted or conveyed. As such, in order to make sure that the message gets through properly, boundary objects are often – as we have argued – accompanied by people.

An easily recognised example of a boundary object is a *disability support notice* (this is the term used at the university where I currently work) – a document, usually consisting of several pages, that outlines the nature of the disability/disabilities of a specific student together with an outline of suggested reasonable adjustments. Such a document is not indigenous to the Community of Disciplinary Practice of which the student is a member, nor will it be absorbed into the repertoire of the community. The function of the document, as a reified form, is to transmit a package of information to the CoP. This information does not affect the joint enterprise or the shared repertoire of the CoP: what it does is inform those members of the CoP who need to know – module tutors and professional services staff – of the reasonable adjustments to the ways in which the student with the disability might engage with the practices of the community. The same documentary process is used for all such notices across the university, irrespective of the types of disabilities being recorded or the kinds of adjustments that are required. As such, the disability support notice is an example of a *standardised form* (Star & Griesemer, 1989).

In situations such as these, boundary objects can act as carriers of meaning or practice that can then travel around between different CoPs, without being permanently absorbed into one of them. In this way, they can help with the circulation of ideas, practices, processes, and so forth. Wenger notes that the use or employment of boundary objects constitutes a form of participation. What he does not address directly is the extent to which boundary objects might need to be accompanied. Here we can consider a further theoretical plug-in (in addition to those discussed in Chapter 5) and draw on the sociology of John Law. Law (1994), in discussing how messages or packages of information might travel across spatial or institutional distances, used the example of a text-based artefact to explore the need for objects to be accompanied by people. A text is a robust form that can travel considerable distances, Law notes, but there is no guarantee as to how it will be received when it arrives at its destination. Moreover, it might be damaged *en route*. Sometimes, a text will need a person to reinforce, defend, or otherwise elucidate the message that it is intended to convey. Law's analysis, which pertains to the broader field of *actor-network theory*, is echoed by the idea of the "literacy sponsor" (Brandt & Clinton, 2002).

Summing Up: Boundaries

- The boundaries of a CoP can be institutional, linguistic, or geographic. It can be based on identifiable practices or more tacit ones.
- Boundaries are always permeable, but different arrangements apply: some communities are straightforward to join, whilst others have more stringent entry requirements.
- Both people and things can travel across boundaries, and this might be temporary or permanent.

Multimembership

CoPs can share routines, processes, ways of knowing, and so forth in different ways, therefore. Sometimes, ways of knowing, artefacts, or habits are permanently copied and absorbed from one CoP to another; at other times, artefacts or processes will visit CoPs, deliver their messages, perhaps make some kind of difference to localised practices, and then move on. CoPs will also host visitors, sometimes looking to establish more permanent connections, but at other times only anticipating a brief sojourn within the destination CoP. Many of us will visit CoPs. Many of us will also be members of multiple CoPs. These *trajectories of multimembership* (Wenger, 1998, pp. 158–160) will overlap in different ways: we might spend a very long time as members of some CoPs but only a short amount of time in others; we might be experts in some and novices in others. We might borrow heavily from one in order to enhance our practice in another. Different patterns of multimembership are possible.

Multimembership of a number of CoPs – they might all belong to the same constellation, but this does not have to be the case – consists of two interacting elements: *identity* and *reconciliation*. When we talk about identity, we have to remember that our identities as people in the (social) world are shaped by all sorts of things, including our differing levels of membership of different CoPs, both in the past (these are our *histories of learning*) and the present. We are different when we are in different places. We speak, behave, and dress differently at work and at home. We might speak differently to different groups of students depending on whether they are first-year or final-year undergraduates, whether they are full-time or part-time, or whether they are international or home students. But we do not build walls between these different parts of our identities. We might tell a story about our own experiences, say, as a way of illustrating a point that we are trying to get across to our students. We might reflect on how a session went with one group of students and then adapt the resources when sitting down with the next group. On one day, we might be working with a longstanding group of students, teaching a curriculum that we know inside-out because we have been running the modules in question for several years and our trajectory is that of the *insider*. And on the next day, we might be working with a new group in a new subject area, on an *inbound* trajectory that reflects our relative lack of professional experience. But all of these CoPs and all of these trajectories remain separate, even though they all work on us, and we are members of them, at the same time. We borrow from one, travel from one to the other, talk differently in some than in others, and so forth. This is what we mean when we talk about our identities as resting on multimembership (Wenger, 1998).

When occupying the *nexus of multimembership*, moving between CoPs or borrowing from one CoP and giving to another can be perfectly straightforward, especially if the CoPs in question are closely aligned. The alignment between different CoPs helps them join together in ways that allow the practices of those CoPs to expand and travel (Wenger, 1998, pp. 178–181). This helps us make the most of the opportunities for learning afforded to us through multimembership (Oborn & Dawson, 2010). Whatever the nature of our engagement in a CoP or the trajectory that we are following, we may find that our practice in one CoP is enhanced, better understood, or ameliorated by drawing on our practice from another. At other times, however, we may find ourselves occupying positions that are contradictory, or that might push us into an action or a process that makes sense from the standpoint of one CoP, but is less agreeable or appropriate to another. On occasions such as this, our identity relies on *reconciliation work*. My own research (Communities of Research Practice are discussed in Chapter 8) as an ethnographer of education has undoubtedly been enhanced as a consequence of my engagement in the related but different field of medical education research. My identity as an academic, by contrast, is more complex to reconcile with my identity as a programme leader or as a member of a departmental senior leadership team or when occupying faculty-level posts (all of which I have done in the past at both my current and previous institutions). For anyone who has found it sometimes difficult to balance "academic" and "management/leadership" roles, who has had to work hard to reconcile philosophies of research with research policies driven by audit cultures, or who has found their own identity and subjectivity under pressure from the social and cultural conditions of the university as workplace, such tensions will be all too familiar (Beattie, 2020; Leathwood & Read, 2013; Teelken, 2011).

Constellations of Communities of Practice

Discussions about multimembership and reconciliation, boundaries, and brokers necessarily lead us to consider the ways in which *constellations* of CoPs – arrangements of different CoPs that can be more or less tightly bound – work together. For Wenger, Alinsu – the medical claims organisation where he carried out his ethnographic research – is quite clearly a constellation: it is too diffuse to be considered a single CoP but instead can be seen as being made up of a number of CoPs that share elements of practice, of ways of working and talking, forms and artefacts, and so forth (Wenger, 1998, p. 127). Wenger also goes on to suggest that a school is a constellation of CoPs: so why not a university?

Whether or not we see disciplines and departments or programmes of study and modules or interdisciplinary and cross-disciplinary institutes as CoPs, it is simple enough to imagine how they might be arranged as a constellation. Different departments face similar conditions (competing for resources and for students, responding to the Research Excellence Framework), share a geographical and/or institutional proximity (a single university with two campuses, one in a different city or even country, is still a single constellation), often have both people and resources in common (technicians, libraries, virtual learning environments), and share both historical and current enterprises (the doing of research, the doing of university teaching, and so forth). From this standpoint, describing an entire university as a single CoP becomes difficult because the scope and scale of the practices being subsumed are simply too varied to be encompassed within a single entity. To describe a university as a constellation, by contrast, makes more sense. It is self-evidently an institutional entity with a common, if diffuse, body of shared *joint enterprises* with sufficient commonalities to treat them as a single unit of analysis when required. Likewise, there are many commonly held formats and processes for *mutual engagement* whether relating to teaching (annual teaching and learning conferences for staff), research (university research and ethics committees), or indeed any of the other cross-institutional functions of a university (internationalisation strategies, Athena Swan and Race Equality Charter submissions, admissions, and clearing). As constellations can be more or less tightly bound, we can therefore recognise how there may be more activity between some CoPs as opposed to others, whilst still all remaining within the same constellation.

Within a constellation, the work done by brokers and visitors across different boundaries likewise becomes recognisable. Internal quality assurance panels draw people from different disciplines – different CoPs – together on a temporary basis to discuss academic matters that will be more or less familiar to the members of the panel depending on the proximity of their "home" CoPs to that which is under review. Faculty-level meetings of heads of departments will allow the distinct concerns or problems faced by an individual departmental CoP to be rehearsed and perhaps resolved in a context where these problems might be seen, mediated by specific and local concerns, as being present or latent in other CoPs within the faculty. Institutional research policies, a form of boundary object, will need to be agreed upon with representatives from different departmental and/or faculty offices and then circulated across the entire constellation. And like any such textual object, it may require people to explain it and/or defend it. Learning and teaching conferences provide opportunities for university teachers to share aspects of their pedagogic practice – part of the *shared repertoire* of their own departments – across boundaries: more closely aligned CoPs – anthropology and archaeology – will be able to share more, and more profoundly, than will more distant CoPs across the constellation such as chemistry and music.

In order to facilitate practices such as these, people will take on roles as brokers and visitors, bringing people and practices together in different formations. Some of these will be frequent and relatively durable, such as research committee meetings, whilst others will be durable but less frequent such as an all-staff conference. More durable formations may possess greater powers of persuasion and influence to encourage participation. Other formations – working groups, staff interest groups – may be less durable, perhaps by design, perhaps because there are fewer forces/pressures that require and/or persuade people to engage, or perhaps because the commonalities in enterprise or repertoire that first brought them together are only temporary. Members of staff will take on – sometimes quite willingly, but at other times through a sense of obligation – different brokering or visiting roles, sometimes also drawing on and/or enhancing their nexuses of multimembership, circulating through the constellation, accompanied by artefacts and agendas, and facilitated by processes and persuasion.

Summing Up: Multimembership and Constellations

- Multimembership allows us to explain how we can carry our ways of knowing from one CoP to another, recontextualising our practice as we cross boundaries.
- CoPs are never isolated: they are always arranged in constellations. Sometimes these will be highly diffuse, whilst at other times they will be more tightly bound.

Becoming a Professional Youth Worker: Negotiations Across Constellations

Our former student, now a newly qualified youth worker, has travelled through several of the component CoPs of one constellation – the constellation that encompasses the university at which they studied – and has now embarked upon a new trajectory into a new constellation, based around the organisation that they are working in. The different university CoPs have – thanks to their shared elements of practice, of repertoire, of engagement, and so forth – given our student the opportunity, through multimembership, of coming to know about a number of different aspects of youth work practice, both academic and professional. The university and the profession occupy distinct constellations, but these are nonetheless linked together in a variety of forms and through several different means in just the same way that the communities internal to each constitution are linked. The professional constellation, as it were, informs the practices of the academic constellation in several ways: the professional standards frame the academic curriculum and provide a public-facing endorsement of the programme through accreditation; professional ways of knowing are recontextualised in the academic curriculum; aspects of the discourses of the profession find their way into the university; placement opportunities are co-opted into the formal assessment of the degree scheme; entry into the professional constellation is accomplished through the award of a degree certificate – a boundary object that carries meaning from one constellation to the next. Travel between CoPs within these two constellations is facilitated and controlled by a number of different people: brokers (open-day advisers and recruitment managers); experts (academic staff, university placement officers); and visitors (guest lecturers, mentors). Our former student has, simply put, traversed a series of CoPs across constellations, following a series of variously unbound and outbound trajectories, learning through practice and through multimembership, becoming used to and then using the discourses of university youth work but also of professional youth work, and taking on a succession of identities firstly as a youth work student and subsequently as a youth work professional, all the while negotiating the different meanings that reify their academic and professional learning.

Conclusion: Boundaries Within and Beyond Constellations

Moving across and between different CoPs is, I would argue, typical of pretty much everyone who works in higher education. We change jobs, participate in committee work, act as external examiners, and take on cross-departmental management and leadership roles. We visit colleagues, collaborate in writing papers, and deliver research seminars. Sometimes, these boundary crossings can be difficult to accomplish and hard to acknowledge. At other times, boundary crossing is something that, as individual community members, we prioritise, acknowledging that our interests and passions reside in boundary work rather than the more central work of the community. However it happens and for whatever reason, the movement of both people and things across boundaries is a common, even necessary, aspect of the practice of any community which in turn helps to establish and sustain a constellation of communities. CoPs need new people and new artefacts, sometimes to absorb and call their own, sometimes to provide an injection of novelty, offer a note of concern, provide some constructive criticism, or simply to hold a friendly conversation. It would require a highly complex diagram to map out all of the CoPs in just one university, let alone a national or even international sector. But what we can do is trace the constellations of CoPs that we are enrolled in as teachers and as researchers, in order to make sense of the different directions that we have to travel and the different ways in which we are sometimes pushed.

References

Beattie, L. (2020). Educational leadership: Producing docile bodies? A Foucauldian perspective on higher education. *Higher Education Quarterly*, 74(1), 98–110.

Belfiore, M., Defoe, T., Folinsbee, S., Hunter, J., & Jackson, N. (2004). *Reading work: Literacies in the new workplace*. Lawrence Erlbaum Associates.

Boud, D., & Middleton, H. (2003). Learning from others at work: Communities of practice and informal learning. *Journal of Workplace Learning*, 15(5), 194–202.

Brandt, T., & Clinton, K. (2002). Limits of the local: Expanding perspectives on literacy as a social practice. *Journal of Literacy Research*, 34(3), 337–356.

Eraut, M. (1994). *Developing professional knowledge and competence*. RoutledgeFalmer.

Law, J. (1994). *Organising modernity*. Blackwell.

Leathwood, C., & Read, B. (2013). Research policy and academic performativity: Compliance, contestation and complicity. *Studies in Higher Education*, 38(8), 1162–1174.

Oborn, E., & Dawson, S. (2010). Learning across communities of practice: An examination of multidisciplinary work. *British Journal of Management*, 21(4), 843–858.

Star, S. L., & Griesemer, J. (1989). Institutional ecology, 'translations' and boundary objects: Amateurs and professionals in Berkeley's Museum of vertebrate zoology, 1907–39. *Social Studies of Science*, 19(3), 387–420.

Teelken, C. (2011). Compliance or pragmatism: How do academics deal with managerialism in higher education? A comparative study in three countries. *Studies in Higher Education*, 37(3), 271–290.

Weller, A. (2017). Professional associations as communities of practice: Exploring the boundaries of ethics and compliance and corporate social responsibility. *Business and Society Review*, 122(3), 359–392.

Wenger, E. (1998). *Communities of practice: Learning, meaning and identity*. Cambridge University Press.

Chapter 7

Assessment Within a Community of Practice

Introduction

In this chapter, I am going to explain how we can make sense of assessment as an aspect of the shared repertoire of any Community of Practice (CoP) within higher education where one of the objects of practice is centred around the formal and documented learning of university students – a Community of Pedagogic Practice. From the point of view of early expressions of the theories of situated learning in communities of practice, assessment is, arguably, antithetical to any CoP, symbolising as it does the characteristics of formal structures of educational provision based on individualistic and positivistic models of cognition and intelligence that Jean Lave, in particular, was opposed to. However, the later ideas of Etienne Wenger provide a way through which we can insert the practices of assessment – including feedback – as essential components of any Community of Pedagogic Practice. If this is done carefully we can maintain the integrity of the CoP framework whilst at the same time expanding somewhat on the design of the Learning Architecture that we have already explored.

Communities of Pedagogic Practice

Up to now, we have considered ways in which CoPs can be framed as academic disciplines. This approach makes sense (as explained in Chapter 2) but nonetheless can cause some difficulties when we consider the different practices of the two most conspicuous cohorts of members of such communities: staff and students. This is because we need to be able to make sense of their differing levels of engagement and participation, and their different trajectories.

Within a CoP, it is far from uncommon to find academic staff who are newcomers working with longer-serving colleagues, alongside undergraduates – on differing trajectories and with differing amounts of experience within the programme – and postgraduates. At one level, it is self-evidently the case that within this – or any – community, the practices of academics will be qualitatively different to those of students. Academics draw on their wider disciplinary knowledge to design and teach a curriculum whilst students study the curriculum – but they rarely have the opportunity to shape it in any meaningful sense (except in relatively minor ways such as when a staff-student consultation process leads to changes in assessment and feedback format). Students write essays and reports, and academics grade them and write feedback. Some students aspire to full participation, to become the next generation of academics. Other students adopt a much more strategic or instrumental approach to their studies: not all peripheral participants aspire to full participation. The trajectories followed by staff and students are so diverse, their respective modes of work are so different in relation to the academic discipline, that for some theorists it becomes difficult if not impossible to envisage a single community that can satisfactorily encompass these distinct practices. For other writers, the different positions of staff and students need to be understood in terms of membership of the same CoPs but following different paths or trajectories, rather than in terms of membership of different CoPs (Ashwin, 2009). Leaving aside these different possible arrangements of CoPs for a moment, a further problem is that even though CoPs rest on a particular understanding of learning – as social practice, as legitimate peripheral participation – there is, as the theory was first described, no place within them for students as distinct from teachers. This is the *pedagogy problem* in CoP theory (Tummons, 2014), which was addressed in Chapter 3. We can reconcile pedagogy with CoP theory and situated learning, therefore. But we still have to decide where, within a Community of Higher Education Practice, pedagogy can be located.

In this chapter and the next, I am going to resolve this problem by bifurcating the practices of teaching and research, despite having accepted these as two defining features of disciplinary work within higher education that are linked in many ways in what has been described in conceptual terms such as the teaching-research nexus (Clark & Hordosy, 2019) as well as through commonly found constructions such as "research-led teaching" and "research-informed teaching". I propose that an academic discipline can be described in terms of not one but two distinct, though heavily intermingled, CoPs: one based around research, and the other based around teaching. In this way we can reconcile the different kinds of work – the practices – done on the one hand by lecturers and professors – and research/dissertation students – when doing research, and on the other hand by lecturers and professors when they are teaching or assessing and by students when they are doing the everyday work of being a student. We can see this as an example of *reconciliation work*, and draw on ideas about *multimembership* (as discussed in the previous chapter), in order to position academics and students as having, for the purposes of this discussion, (at least) two distinct but sometimes overlapping identities. One of these identities revolves around research work; the other revolves around the work of learning and teaching. And each of these is situated within two closely aligned and overlapping – but nonetheless distinct – CoPs.

One of these is a Community of Research Practice, and these will be discussed in the following chapter. The other is a Community of Pedagogic Practice (Blanton & Stylianou, 2009; Brandon & Charlton, 2011; Houghton et al., 2015; Laksov et al., 2008).

There are several aspects of formal educational provision that, irrespective of the enrolment status of the students, are visible to the rest of the world, and in their own ways, these help to mark out or signify the *boundaries* of Communities of Pedagogic Practice. Many of these are already familiar to us: the actual places – the buildings, or areas of buildings – where educational provision happens; the uniforms and lanyards worn by students (as well as staff); the certificates – the all-important *boundary objects* that students take with them when they leave. But even though we have discussed how a certificate travels from one constellation of CoPs to another and allows the holder to cross over boundaries into new CoPs, we still need to work out how the certificate actually came into existence in the first place – the processes of participation that lead to reification. In order to do this, we need to think about the assessment processes that all come together and lead up to the generating of a certificate. But we can't do that without first thinking about assessment as an aspect of pedagogical practice that somehow slots into a CoP. This will require some careful thinking. We have found a way to resolve the *pedagogy problem* within CoP. What we now have to do is to solve a related problem – the *assessment problem* – in order to find ways to locate assessment within a Community of Pedagogic Practice. Assessment needs to be reconciled to the *joint enterprise* of the CoP, described in terms of *shared repertoire*, and accomplished through particular aspects of *mutual engagement*.

Our first step is to think about social practice accounts of assessment – research and writing that explores assessment not from the point of view of psychology or psychometrics, cognitive load or learning gain (all of which are of course open to critique) but in terms of the everyday stuff that people do in order for assessment to happen. In doing so, we will be able to see how a social practice theory of assessment is a further example of a *theoretical plug-in* (as discussed in Chapter 3) that can fit into CoP theory quite neatly. The second step will require us to come at the *assessment problem* from the other direction, as it were, to return to CoP theory and to use it as the basis for a 'native' solution to the problem. Once we have taken these two steps, more familiar aspects of assessment theory – in particular *validity* and *reliability* – will fall into place within the CoP framework. And finally, with one further element of CoP theory added from Wenger (1998), we will be able to explain how certificates come into being and account for the work that they do.

Assessment as a Social Practice

Thinking about assessment as social practice means focussing on those different things that people – university students and teachers, external examiners, secretaries to exam boards – do that are about or related to the work of assessment in a broad sense. For example, when thinking about portfolio-based assessment – a common assessment format across many professional curricula – we might think about the ways in which an individual student might go about the work of collecting together the different materials that they need to satisfy the assessment requirements of any one element of the curriculum (Trevitt et al., 2011). For any assessment, whether a portfolio or a performance piece, a coursework essay or a timed examination paper, one important quality is *validity* – does the assessment actually assess the content that it sets out to assess, and does the assessment process provide a justification for the ways in which the assessment results will be used? Perhaps unsurprisingly, there are different ways of researching and theorising assessment validity. One approach might be to measure assessment validity through the analysis of examination results in order to establish the *validity coefficient* of the examination in question. If we are going to think about assessment validity from a social practice standpoint, however, we might not necessarily look to measure validity in this way, but instead to account for how we arrived at a definition of validity in the first place in terms of a shared sociocultural understanding of the term and then, more importantly, how different people make sense of assessment validity and then use their understanding of validity to shape their assessment practices and decisions ranging from grading and feedback to drawing up marking criteria.

Social practice accounts of assessment help us to foreground the kinds of stories that get lost sight of when we read the reports written by external examiners, or when we contemplate a long list of yet-to-be-graded assignments within the virtual learning environment for our module. Quality assurance processes describe assessment work in ways that suggest that everything is sufficient, valid, and reliable: results are checked two or even three times; the work of different markers has been second marked and internally moderated, all the while in reference to appropriate assessment benchmarks – a series of practices that look to establish a robust alignment between quality and curriculum requirements on the one hand, and assessment activity (writing assessments grading, second marking and so forth) on the other. Social practice research tells us something rather different, however. It informs us that assessment is sufficient, valid, and reliable *enough* but that the processes that get us to this point are far from straightforward, and will never be complete: an assessment task is never "completely" valid or "perfectly" reliable. Meanwhile, fine-grained explorations of assessment practices soon dispel any notions of unproblematic objectivity and demonstrate the many subjectivities, improvisations and recourses to tacit understandings of procedure that invariably characterise university assessment and grading practices (Hudson et al., 2017; O'Donovan et al. (2024) irrespective of whether or not the person doing the marking is a novice or an expert (Ecclestone, 2001).

The theoretical standpoint taken here relating to assessment involves an understanding of the work of marking student submissions, writing feedback, agreeing grades with colleagues, form-filling and so forth as sociocultural practices. As such, they need to be learned through Legitimate Peripheral Participation, reified through participation (assessment boards are a specific form of participation, mark sheets are a specific form of reification), discussed within other CoPs when required (when reporting to faculty or university-level education committees) and acknowledged as situated within particular departments and disciplines as CoPs. There are many commonalities, but assessment is as situated, as particular to a particular sociocultural context, as is anything else.

Having established that we can shift our point of view by thinking about assessment as a social practice, we are now in a position to bring things into even sharper focus, and describe assessment in terms of one specific social practice theory – CoP. We need to draw on some specific elements of CoP theory and map them to a theoretical understanding of assessment and to evaluate the ways in which CoP theory has already been used to make sense of assessment within higher education.

Assessment in a Community of Practice

We have resolved the *pedagogy problem* and begun thinking of ways in which we can reconcile a mode of instruction with a theoretical framework for explaining learning in social contexts that resolutely rejects formal pedagogical practices and resources. Assessment likewise poses problems from the point of view of anyone subscribing to an unaltered use of Lave and Wenger's work. Formal assessment practices involving evaluations of students' assessment performances by university teachers, the creation of procedures and resources in order to facilitate such an evaluation cycle, and the involvement by students in the construction of material objects of any kind or in the performance of specified tasks that have only been brought into being in the first place in order to complete the assessment task, are all incompatible with the ideas expressed in situated learning theory (Lave & Wenger, 1991). If you are busy generating stuff in order to demonstrate your capacity or competence, you are *not* axiomatically engaged *in* the practice of the CoP, but you *are* generating materials that are *about* the practice of the CoP. Legitimate Peripheral Participation (LPP) is not, we remember, a "pedagogical strategy or a teaching technique" but a model of learning which happens "no matter which educational form provides a context for learning, or whether there is *any* educational form at all" (Lave & Wenger, 1991, p. 40 – emphasis added). For Lave and Wenger, there are "conflicts between learning to know and learning to display knowledge for evaluation" (Lave & Wenger, 1991, 112). A subscription to LPP and CoP theories therefore entails a profound rejection of formal assessment.

A *Learning Architecture* provides us with a framework for pedagogy and for formal instruction, but still without a clear statement as to how assessment might be part of this framework (an understandable *lacuna*, since Wenger's main focus is not on the explication of educational institutions such as universities, notwithstanding his clear interest in educational structures (Wenger, 1998, pp. 263–277). Assuming that we all subscribe to the view that assessment of whatever kind is an unavoidable element of higher education provision (although there are a number of scholars who would disagree), our first steps are to consider those aspects of CoP theory that might help us make sense of assessment before turning to the work done by other scholars who have drawn on CoP theory in order to accomplish similar ends.

The Participation and Reification of Assessment Practices

The linked concepts of *participation* and *reification* (Wenger, 1998, pp. 55–62) are vital to any attempt to insert a theory of assessment into CoP, and although we have touched on this dualism already in Chapter 4, it requires some further exploration here. Participation is relatively straightforward, and refers to the process of taking part in something. However, Wenger reserves the concept of participation for the *people* who are members of a CoP: an apprentice participates in the practice of the community, but the *tools* or *object* that they might use do not participate: they are used, employed, adjusted, or modified by the participants. Participation in practice is what allows our apprentice to engage in learning through LPP, to follow particular *trajectories*, grow and shift their *identities*, and so forth.

The process of reification is linked to participation and is fundamental to any CoP. When we reify something we take something that is an abstract or mental thing and convert it into a physical one. The decision to reify something renders aspects of that thing in a concrete (though not necessarily physical) form, but it does not follow that a reification lasts forever. Artefacts need to be properly used and maintained, kept from harm, circulated appropriately, and so forth. Dealing with reifications is not straightforward. We can see that it is not possible to capture perfectly the thing that we had as an abstract thing when we convert it into a concrete one. Discussions about marking university-level assignments, reified within marking criteria, are hard (if not impossible) to capture in a concrete form that is unequivocal in meaning and intent. What do we mean when we describe an essay as "outstanding" as opposed to "excellent"? Is an 'appropriate use of resources' the same across different academic disciplines? Any reified form, therefore, is always *partial* – it only captures some of whatever it is that is being converted into a solid form. We can also see that once we have got a reified form, it does not follow that everyone will automatically use, read, or interpret it *in the same way*. This profound aspect of reification explains the necessity for moderation meetings, trial marking exercises, second marking, external examination and so forth: our published assessment criteria – as text-based reifications – are inherently prone to ambiguities in understanding and therefore need to be accompanied by other processes and practices to help with the negotiation of their meaning. And this is a negotiation that will always be situated and therefore local.

If reifications are inherently less-than-perfect representations of more complicated mental or abstract topics, discussions and ideas, and are also less-than-perfect because they are inherently capable of being misinterpreted or misread, then how should we make sense of what they do more generally? The answer to this lies in thinking about the relationship between any reified thing, and the people who are going to use it in some way. The work that a reification can or might do can only be understood once we remember that we need at least one person to help with that work. A book cannot read itself; a tool cannot pick itself up; a PDF file cannot email itself. Within CoP theory, reified objects *always* need some people to help them do what they do. Someone needs to pick up a book and turn the pages, open the PDF file on screen, pick up the tool and apply it to the correct process. Some people may then disagree with or even ignore what they are reading, and move to something else; other people will discard the tool that they have selected and use a different one. Alternatively, someone might be so inspired by what they read that they change aspects of their practice, or use the tool in order to come to a profound understanding of a specific operational technique or body of abstracted knowledge for the first time. The way in which we engage in practice within our communities rests on any number of reifications. Some of these will have been around for a long time and others will be new. We might create some of these and adjust or modify others. Some might be used frequently and others might get ignored, rendered obsolete, or left behind. Any kind of object or artefact within a CoP is a reification – something that started out as an idea and has now been made into a tangible, practical thing, and it is through our participation in practice that they are activated – brought into use – or deactivated – put to one side. And this is why, as we have already seen, participation and reification form a dualism.

CoP theory provides us with two further theoretical components that can help us to think critically and carefully about how text-based artefacts are created and used. Of greatest relevance to a discussion of assessment and feedback are *transparency* and *communicative ability*. Transparency relates to the interplay between the use of any artefact and the understanding of why it is important or significant. As someone's participation becomes more full, so artefacts become more transparent to the practitioner (Lave & Wenger, 1991, pp. 101–102). The more we learn, the more easily we can use the artefacts. In part, this is simply because we know more and therefore we can engage in practice in a more extensive manner: we can do more stuff. And in part it is because as we know more, we are better able to understand the full significance or utility of any of the resources of the community, including texts. Wenger develops this further through the concept of the communicative ability of an artefact (Wenger, 1998, p. 64). Communicative ability rests on two factors: the extent to which a CoP member understands the significance of the artefact as a consequence of the extent or depth of her/his participation; and the extent to which an artefact manages to embody meaning. Thus, the negotiation of meaning pertaining to any artefact within a CoP also rests on the participation/reification dualism.

This same participation/reification dualism informs our understanding of the practices engaged in by students within their Communities of Disciplinary Practice as they complete their assessed work, therefore, irrespective of the modality or genre of that assessment. "Standard" academic essays, reports, installations, portfolios, performances and reflective journals are all reifications that are brought into being as a necessary aspect of the students' participation, as are feedback forms, moderation reports, pass lists, and so on and so forth. Assessment is just one example of a practice that is suffused with text-based reifications. And it is as varied as the different curricula found across the HE sector.

Empirical Explorations of Assessment Using Communities of Practice

The volume of published research papers that explore aspects of assessment and feedback practice in higher education is considerable: the number that utilise CoP theory is much smaller by comparison and, as is the case with the CoPs in HE literature more broadly, theory-use is variable and not always meaningful, by which I mean to stress that the explanatory and predictive potential of CoP theory is not always realised. That said there are several well-informed empirical explorations of aspects of assessment practice in higher education that use CoP as a lens through which to make sense of their findings, and these are worth noting.

In a paper from 2005, Margaret Price draws on CoP theory in order to investigate the tensions that exist between attempts to generate sector-wide benchmarks for undergraduate assessment on the one hand, and local (that is, departmental rather than institutional) marking and feedback practices on the other. Her inquiry is driven by the simple question: how do university teachers come to know about assessment standards? Price frames her discussion in terms of the social relationships that are a necessary aspect of such a 'coming to know' process, and uses CoP theory to investigate the gap between the proliferation of criteria and descriptors, and the subjective practices of the assessors for whom these have been constructed. This gap has frequently been accounted for in terms of the differences between tacit and explicit knowledge, or espoused theory and theory-in-use. For Price, drawing on CoP theory, it is situated in the *joint enterprise* of the business school where she conducted her empirical work. More specifically, she posits an "assessment community of practice" (Price, 2005, p. 226) as the location for such work, and proposes that an assessment standards discourse (Price, 2005) is needed if a common view of assessment standards is to be established. It is due to insufficient engagement with this CoP that excessive variance in assessment understanding emerges. Although she does not make this link, it is unproblematic to propose – I suggest – that such a discourse would therefore form part of the *shared repertoire* of such a CoP.

Nicola Reimann and Angelina Wilson are similarly focussed on the ways in which CoP theory can help illuminate assessment practices that are otherwise perceived in tacit, rather than explicit, terms. Their work is focussed on an exploration of an institution-wide initiative that has set out to foreground greater understanding and application of the principles of *Assessment for Learning* (AfL) in higher education (Reimann & Wilson, 2012). The unit of inquiry is a cross-institutional CoP that has been formed specifically to unpack and then advance the use of AfL principles across the university. The participants, not themselves versed in CoP theory, discussed their engagement in the AfL programme in terms of the benefits for the students of the authenticity of assessment within the AfL paradigm, and the value of having a space in which to share experiences and ideas about assessment practice. Reimann and Wilson, using a CoP lens, describe their participants' experiences as an example of a widening of shared repertoire, with the participants finding time to reflect on their own understanding, share this with people from beyond their usual institutional settings, before carrying what they have learned from the AfL CoP (as it were) to their home departments, thereby acting as brokers and subsequently being able to make meaningful changes to existing assessment processes.

Ian Herbert, John Joyce and Trevor Hassall share with Price (2005) a concern for processes of standardisation of assessment practice, and alignment of assessment decisions, which they explore in terms of assessment reliability. They conducted interview-based research into a markers' standardisation meeting for a professional accounting programme and focussed on three areas of activity: moderation to ensure inter-rater reliability, the clarity of understanding of the assessment tasks being marked, and the nature and content of the professional discussions that took place, in order to address the question: *what* is being standardised in standardisation meetings? Drawing on Wenger's concepts of participation, reification and negotiation of meaning, they describe the standardisation meeting as a locus for the negotiation of shared meaning with the marking scheme as the key reification around which the participation of the markers is situated. They go on to identify three aspects of practice within this community of markers: the inculcation of new members into the marking practices of the community, the practice of shared marking in order to establish shared understanding of the criteria, and conversations that encourage not only shared understanding of the criteria but also shared meaning-making in relation to the principles of assessment underpinning the curriculum more broadly (Herbert et al., 2014). The salience of this research for the higher education sector resides in the authors' assertion that such professional marking communities ought to be utilised to a much greater extent than is currently the case by universities – in essence (although Herbert and colleagues do not employ the term) arguing for the establishment of new patterns of *brokerage* between professional and academic communities.

The reliable application of assessment criteria and marking rubrics is also a focus for inquiry by Peter Grainger and colleagues in their investigation of assessment practices more generally within a teacher education curriculum. The specific focus of their research – based on interviews with academics and on the textual analysis of relevant curriculum documentation – are the *grading tools* employed across several different programmes (undergraduate and postgraduate), which are used by the students for self-assessment and reflection, and by the teachers when making their assessment decisions (Grainger et al., 2017). Using the practitioner model of CoPs (Wenger et al., 2002), Grainger et al. discuss what they describe as a CoP formation around the work of doing assessment with the grading tools, characterised by "authentic discussions that facilitated the development of knowledge" (Grainger et al., 2017, p. 412). It is in the writing of or, better, the reification of (although this terminology is not used in the paper) the different assessment-facing documents that the interest lies. Grainger et al. offer two main conclusions in relation to these textual artefacts. Firstly, they foreground the (growing) importance of alignment between different document elements (such as task descriptors versus assessment criteria) in order to ensure clarity of understanding for the reader – student and teacher. And secondly, they discuss the importance of choice of words and expressions and explore terminology that should be used and terminology that should be avoided.

These four studies are situated in different institutional contexts and focus on different student cohorts across different curricula. What they share is a concern to address the phenomenon "that tools designed to increase transparency through the provision of explicit criteria and grade descriptors do little to improve understanding of standards by staff or students" (Price, 2005, p. 217), a statement that rings true after two decades of research and writing, staff development, promotions of constructs such as research literacy, curricular and institutional initiatives such as student-as-partner, renewed focuses on self-assessment and peer assessment, and so forth. The understanding of criteria by both staff and students, notwithstanding the proliferation of documentation that surrounds assessment more broadly (certainly a good example of documentism (Wenger et al., 2002, p. 147)), constitutes a wicked problem as well as a persistent one. Could a more extensive application of CoP theory help explain – if not resolve – this problem?

Theoretical Explorations of Assessment Using Communities of Practice

Of the relatively small number of academic papers or chapters that have explored assessment from a CoP perspective, only a very few embrace the theoretical challenges posed by the *assessment problem*. By this I mean to take a step back from the standpoint shared by papers such as those four just discussed to consider a more profound question: what is assessment within a CoP? Papers such as those referred to above pose a number of useful and theoretically well-informed questions for us as higher education researchers, but they do not problematise fully the position or condition of assessment as a sociocultural practice within a CoP. The presence of assessment is assumed and then critiqued in much the same way as the presence of teaching, of a discourse of pedagogy, is normalised within many CoP-informed accounts of (higher) education practice. But what we also need is to be able to theorise assessment as an element of CoP work more broadly. It is self-evidently the case that forms of at least informal assessment and evaluation must be present in any CoP, not least reified in the ways that experts/old-timers talk to novices/newcomers about the practices that the latter are engaging with on a peripheral basis.

In a (for me, essential) paper published over 20 years ago, Thomas Rømer addresses head-on the challenge to assessment theory and practice posed by the theory of situated learning within CoP. Any consideration of assessment within a CoP constitutes a profound theoretical challenge when we remember that the starting point expressed by Lave and Wenger was that due to the situated nature of ways of knowing within a CoP, it is impossible on an epistemological basis to demonstrate any kind of knowledge outside the CoP, irrespective of the purpose (in this case, assessment) of the demonstration. Rømer resolves this problem by drawing on Wenger's notion of a CoP as being, amongst other things, a "regime of competence" (Wenger, 1998, p. 137), where competence is widely interpreted as being "the distinctions that are given credit by the community" (Rømer, 2002, p. 238). Following Rømer we can therefore understand assessment as another element of the shared repertoire of any CoP, enacted through particular patterns of mutual engagement, and necessarily aligned to the joint enterprise of the community. It is the way by which newcomers/apprentices within the CoP are able to show, and are required to show, to the CoP at large that they are doing things the right way – the way in which the newcomers are required to demonstrate knowing and competence to experts/old-timers; in whatever manner that the more or less complex and multiple ways of knowing situated within the community might need be expressed or displayed in a legitimate – that is to say, authentic, manner. He argues that:

> ... the condition for assessment and evaluation in the traditional interpretation of full participation is the assessor's knowledge of, and ability to relate to, the canonical texts of a tradition and his (sic) general integration in a community.
>
> (Rømer, 2002, p. 238)

We can expand the notion of 'canonical texts' in order to prevent a literalist reading and take this to include any and all aspects of the things that need to be known/done/talked about/practiced within the community. At the same time we need to remember that a Community of Pedagogical Practice in higher will have reified these within the curriculum – an undoubtedly important textual artefact (if not strictly qualifying as a 'canonical text'). With this slight refinement, we can see how Rømer's conclusion allows assessment to be slotted into a CoP, with the experience and expertise – the authenticity – of the assessor as a necessary precondition.

Drawing on Wenger and also on Rømer, we can locate pedagogy and assessment within CoPs by taking three interlinked steps. Firstly, it is possible to locate a discourse of instruction within a CoP and as with any other form of discourse within a CoP, and this should be understood as being a component of shared repertoire (Wenger, 1998). Within a CoP, members with greater expertise in relation to particular practices (often but not axiomatically longer-standing members) inform, demonstrate and explain to other members with lesser expertise in those practices (often but not axiomatically newcomers) how those same practices need to be accomplished. This might involve practicing – and therefore learning – a new technical process, how to write up an analysis in a certain style or genre, how to use a hitherto unfamiliar concept, how to utilise a particular solution or precedent, the name of a specified procedure, and so forth. Any aspect of the joint enterprise of any CoP might be explained or taught through mutual engagement. It is in the authentic and situated expertise of the person giving instruction that the legitimacy of their pedagogical function resides (Rømer, 2002).

Secondly, it is possible to locate assessment within a CoP. Here, I make a distinction between formal and informal assessment (whilst noting that within CoP theory there is no distinction between formal and informal learning) rather than formative and summative assessment, as a reflection of the complicated, not to say contested, boundaries between formative and summative – an argument that has been extensively rehearsed (Broadbent et al., 2017; Harlen & James, 1997; Knight, 2002). I use informal/formal to indicate whether or not any particular form of assessment – observation, judgement, appreciation – is being carried out for the purposes of formal accreditation, recording, certification and so forth. Informal assessment, therefore, can be seen as an aspect of the *shared repertoire* of the CoP (Wenger, 1998), another everyday element of practice through which the longer-standing members of the CoP evaluate, monitor and sense check the practices of relative newcomers (Rømer, 2002). Formal assessment can be made sense of as an example of assessment that in turn generates processes to allow some kind of reification of assessment – a certificate or transcript – to travel between CoPs (as discussed in the previous chapter).

Thirdly, the authenticity and hence validity of assessment (and I shall return to validity shortly) is mediated by the alignment of these assessment practices to the legitimate (peripheral) practice of the community. Authenticity and legitimacy are axiomatic elements of practice, and as such it follows that since all learning within a CoP happens through LPP, and LPP also axiomatically rests on authentic practice, then the validity of the assessment must be found in the relationship or *intersubjectivity* between the student and the teacher as mediated firstly by their trajectory positions within the CoP and secondly by their differently-embodied experience and expertise acquired through their *histories of participation* (Lave & Wenger, 1991; Wenger, 1998). If accreditation is sought – if the assessment process will lead to some form of formal record and certification – then the observation and assessment of the bodies of knowing and expertise being learned will additionally be evaluated by authentically experienced and knowledgeable expert members of other CoPs, acting as brokers in roles such as external examiners, or shadow markers.

Summing Up: Assessment and Communities of Practice

- Assessment can be understood as an element of the shared repertoire of any Community of Pedagogical Practice.
- Feedback is a form of discourse within the CoP and hence also part of the shared repertoire.
- Assessment can be informal and formal. Formal assessment leads to a process of certification/reification.
- The validity of assessment rests on the authenticity of the assessed practice in relation to the practice of the community more broadly, and the intersubjectivity of the assessor and assessee.
- Negotiating understanding of assessment and feedback is contingent on the communicative ability of the assessment artefacts in question.

Assessment Theory and Communities of Practice: Validity and Reliability

Validity and reliability are widely discussed within higher education, and there is not enough room here to explore in full the many debates that surround these constructs. For now, it is sufficient to remember that for an assessment to be valid, it must assess the actual body of knowing that the course or programme of study sets out to deliver, provide sufficient coverage of the content of the course, and be appropriate to the subjects being studied and assessed. There is a further aspect to assessment validity theory, namely *predictive validity* (the extent to which an assessment task can predict to any degree of accuracy the future performance of the assessment taker), which is frequently addressed within the literature, either as a standalone concept or as part of a unitary model of validity (Newton & Shaw, 2014). However, the rejection of straightforward accounts of the transferability of knowing within a situated learning paradigm renders this aspect of validity troublesome at best. Instead, any conceptualisation of the prediction of future capacity or capability derived from a certification or accreditation process needs to be tempered by the need for ways of knowing to be renegotiated across the boundaries of CoPs (Wenger, 1998). For an assessment to be reliable, the judgements pertaining to it must display consistency, ensuring that personal or environmental factors do not affect the assessment process – as extensively described in the four journal articles discussed earlier in the chapter. Judgements must be consistent: irrespective of who the assessor is and where and when the assessment takes place, the outcome must be the same.

So far so good: but there is still a little more discussion to be had. We have established that learning through Legitimate Peripheral Participation requires meaningful opportunities for newcomers to engage in the *authentic practice* of the community. We also know that we can access further authentic experiences through *brokering* work such as taking up placements or internships. Moreover, we have shown that a learning architecture requires authenticity in all of its resources if it is to generate opportunities for meaningful learning. It is important to note that Lave and Wenger's emphasis on authenticity forms part of their critique of formal educational institutions (1991), but this problem is resolved within a learning architecture: Wenger argues that teachers, as one of the structuring resources of any CoP, need to embody "lived authenticity" and not let this be overshadowed by their "pedagogical and institutional functions" (Wenger, 1998, p. 276). This posits a dynamic relationship between subject specialism and pedagogical knowledge that occupies familiar ground within the higher education research field, and has been explored from several different perspectives in terms of debates around subject matter pedagogies and the teaching-research nexus (Tight, 2016; Vereijken & van der Rijst, 2021).

Finally, we need to turn to the relationship between validity and reliability, not least as the relationship between the two is a frequent topic for discussion within assessment theory. Such discussions tend to be framed by the dynamic push-pull relationship that exists between the two, and so a balance has to be struck. However, within a CoP, there is no correlation between validity and reliability, except insofar as they both rest on authenticity. It is through the lived authenticity of the teacher or trainer, as a more experienced, longer-standing member of the CoP, that legitimacy as an assessor or examiner is established. Their identity as "old-timers" is an educational resource (Wenger, 1998, p. 277) in just the same was as their expertise, engagement and practice are resources. Lave and Wenger may well have rejected any notions of evaluation within a CoP as being an inauthentic representation forced on the learner by any formalised curriculum within an institution (Lave & Wenger, 1991, p. 112), but if we are to accept the apprenticeship metaphor that is at the heart of their work, then at some point it must surely be the case that the more experienced member of the community needs to check in on the work done by a newcomer, to make sure that the work that the newcomer is doing is aligned to the *joint enterprise* of the community, is discussed, practiced, queried and acknowledged through the *mutual engagement* of the community, and draws – in an appropriate and meaningful way – on the *shared repertoire* of the community.

Expertise provides reliability in assessment, therefore. But there are two strands to this. The first is the expertise that pertains to the authentic practice of the discipline; the second pertains to the practice of assessment as a pedagogical form – the understanding of learning outcomes and assessment criteria, the use of the feedback forms, the difference between work that passes and work that fails, and so forth. This second strand is also an aspect of authentic practice, in fact, because it encapsulates aspects of the authentic practice of being a university teacher, as we have already seen. Expertise – the disciplinary-specific ways of knowing and doing that make up the joint enterprise of the CoP – is a further example of a *structuring resource* to be accessed by students, an element of the shared repertoire that students will engage with, at first on a peripheral basis and later, as they follow their trajectories, more fully. Expertise in the practice of assessment pertains to the fullest members of the community – the teachers. For students, this is an aspect of the shared repertoire that they only *very* peripherally engage with: their knowledge of assessment practice within the community is restricted, necessarily, to what they need to do: their assignments, and how they are graded. For the teachers, knowing assessment practice is as important as knowing their discipline because both of these bodies of knowledge are elements of a shared repertoire.

Conclusion: Assessment in Higher Education and Communities of Practice

Assessment is part of the shared repertoire of any Community of Pedagogical Practice. It is a form of participation that involves members of the community in different ways, depending on their trajectories and standpoints. For fuller members – university teachers – assessment is an aspect of practice that they shape to some degree (mindful of the influences of external CoPs from across the higher education constellation). It involves their evaluative judgements about the merits and qualities of the work done by more peripheral members – university students – for whom assessment is an aspect of practice reifying their increasingly full participation. Assessment is rendered valid and reliable through authenticity of participation, but this authenticity needs to be carefully maintained: practices such as generating generic criteria or other forms of documentation that purport to enhance validity and reliability that are not sufficiently aligned to the practice of the community will impair and not enhance this aspect of practice. This is not to say that criteria, benchmarks, and the like should be rejected – but to prevent documentism, they need to be accompanied by authentic opportunities for discussion and participation so that their meanings can be negotiated.

References

Ashwin, P. (2009). *Analysing teaching-learning interactions in higher education: Accounting for structure and agency*. Continuum.

Blanton, M., & Stylianou, D. (2009). Interpreting a community of practice perspective in discipline-specific professional development in higher education. *Innovative Higher Education*, 34(2), 79–92.

Brandon, T., & Charlton, J. (2011). The lessons learned from developing an inclusive learning and teaching community of practice. *International Journal of Inclusive Education*, 15(1), 165–178.

Broadbent, J., Panadero, E., & Boud, D. (2017). Implementing summative assessment with a formative flavour: A case study in a large class. *Assessment & Evaluation in Higher Education*, 43(2), 307–322.

Clark, T., & Hordosy, R. (2019). Undergraduate experiences of the research/teaching nexus across the whole student lifecycle. *Teaching in Higher Education*, 24(3), 412–427.

Ecclestone, K. (2001). "I know a 2:1 when I see it": Understanding criteria for degree classifications in franchised university programmes. *Journal of Further and Higher Education*, 25(3), 301–313.

Grainger, P., Christie, M., Thomas, G., Dole, S., Heck, D., Marshman, M., & Carey, M. (2017). Improving the quality of assessment by using a community of practice to explore the optimal construction of assessment rubrics. *Reflective Practice*, 18(3), 410–422.

Harlen, W., & James, M. (1997). Assessment and learning: Differences and relationships between formative and summative assessment. *Assessment in Education: Principles, Policy and Practice*, 4(3), 365–379.

Herbert, I., Joyce, J., & Hassall, T. (2014). Assessment in higher education: The potential for a community of practice to improve inter-marker reliability. *Accounting Education*, 23(6), 542–561.

Houghton, L., Ruutz, A., Green, W., & Hibbins, R. (2015). I just do not have time for new ideas: Resistance, resonance and micro-mobilisation in a teaching community of practice. *Higher Education Research and Development*, 34(3), 527–540.

Hudson, J., Bloxham, S., den Outer, B., & Price, M. (2017). Conceptual acrobatics: Talking about assessment standards in the transparency era. *Studies in Higher Education*, 42(7), 1309–1323.

Knight, P. (2002). Summative assessment in higher education: Practices in disarray. *Studies in Higher Education*, 27(3), 275–286.

Laksov, K., Mann, S., & Dahlgren, L. (2008). Developing a community of practice around teaching: A case study. *Higher Education Research & Development*, 27(2), 121–132.

Lave, J., & Wenger, E. (1991). *Situated learning: Legitimate peripheral participation*. Cambridge University Press.

Newton, P., & Shaw, S. (2014). *Validity in educational and psychological assessment*. Sage Publications.

O'Donovan, B., Sadler, I., & Reimann, N. (2024). Social moderation and calibration versus codification: A way forward for academic standards in higher education? *Studies in Higher Education*. https://doi.org/10.1080/03075079.2024.2321504

Price, M. (2005). Assessment standards: The role of communities of practice and the scholarship of assessment. *Assessment & Evaluation in Higher Education*, 30(3), 215–230.

Reimann, N., & Wilson, A. (2012). Academic development in 'assessment for learning': The value of a concept and communities of assessment practice. *International Journal for Academic Development*, 17(1), 71–83.

Rømer, T. A. (2002). Situated learning and assessment. *Assessment and Evaluation in Higher Education, 27*(3), 233–241.

Tight, M. (2016). Examining the research/teaching nexus. *European Journal of Higher Education, 6*(4), 293–311.

Trevitt, C., Stocks, C., & Quinlan, K. (2011). Advancing assessment practice in continuing professional learning: Toward a richer understanding of teaching portfolios for learning and assessment. *International Journal for Academic Development, 17*(2), 163–175.

Tummons, J. (2014). Learning architectures and communities of practice in higher education. In J. Huisman, & M. Tight (Eds.), *Theory and method in higher education research II* (pp. 121–139). Emerald Group Publishing Limited.

Vereijken, M., & van der Rijst, R. (2021). Subject matter pedagogy in university teaching: How lecturers use relations between theory and practice. *Teaching in Higher Education, 28*(4), 880–893.

Wenger, E. (1998). *Communities of practice: Learning, meaning and identity.* Cambridge University Press.

Wenger, E., McDermott, R., & Snyder, W. (2002). *Cultivating communities of practice.* Harvard Business School Press.

Chapter 8

Research and Communities of Practices

Introduction

In this chapter, I consider the ways in which the doing of research – arguably one of the two most recognisable elements of working in a university – can be explored through Communities of Practice theory. In order to do this, I shall briefly discuss some examples of prior empirical work that has set out to explain a variety of different aspects of research work – writing for publication, running a research group, building research capacity amongst university staff for whom research is a new element of practice – as well as considering some more speculative theorisation of research within CoPs. As the discussion proceeds, I shall draw on several elements of CoP theory that have been discussed in the chapters preceding this one, before offering some conclusions as to the capacity of CoP theory to be reconciled to the processes of discovery, change and innovation tata re axiomatic to research in higher education.

Higher Education: Multiple Communities of Research Practice?

Over the course of several journal articles and books, Malcolm Tight has spent a number of years describing and critiquing the broader higher education research field, exploring not only the nature of the field of research itself but also the ways in which particular methodological and theoretical approaches or frameworks, including CoPs, have been put to use by researchers (Tight, 2013, 2014, 2015, 2018). In one of the earliest components of this *oeuvre* (Tight, 2004), he set out to evaluate theory use within different areas of research activity: by journal (that is, were some journals more demanding of rigorous theory use than others for publication?); by theme (for example, is research into "student experience" more theoretically-engaged than research into "knowledge"?); and by method/methodology (for example, is phenomenography more or less theoretically rigorous than interview-based research?) The answers to these different questions are interesting and are worth following up. But of far greater salience to the line of discussion that I have been following in this book is his decision to frame this inquiry, and his description of the higher education landscape, through CoPs theory. He describes himself as being a member of several overlapping CoPs, relating to higher education research, lifelong learning research and critical learning research, as well as others at course, departmental, and institutional levels. And he concludes by proposing that "higher education research is not a single CoP but, rather, a series of, somewhat overlapping, CoPs. We might seek to define these communities in terms of the topics they study, the method/ologies they use, the journals they publish in, their disciplinary backgrounds or some combination of these" (Tight, 2004, p. 409). Tight hints at the ways we might understand the mutual engagement, joint enterprise and shared repertoire of these CoPs, but gives relatively little rich detail (understandably, in the confines of a single journal article). But it is a simple exercise to extrapolate that specific journals will pertain to specific research communities as examples of reified forms, or that particular methodologies will more commonly be found in the shared repertoire of some communities in comparison to others.

Other researchers have provided variously smaller-scale and more finely-grained accounts of different aspects of research work. Ng and Pemberton (2013), drawing on the practitioner model of CoPs (Wenger et al., 2002), conducted an interview and observation-based study of research groups across five different areas of the curriculum, (although these research groups did not necessarily identify as CoPs): clinical practice, business and management, English literature, English history, and Information and Communication Technology. Participants spoke about several beneficial aspects of group membership in ways that can be mapped onto CoP theory: as helping foster a sense of belonging and identity, as an informal space/place for learning and training, and as a way of overcoming intellectual isolation. Ng and Pemberton concluded that research-based CoPs such as these, involving both senior and junior academics, benefit both individual researchers and the institution that houses them, and offer particular benefits for individuals at different stages of their careers in terms of research ability. A similar analysis was conducted by Degn et al. (2018) who revisited their earlier empirical studies of different research groups – in chemistry, theoretical physics, biomedicine and the social sciences – in order to explore the extent to which they might be considered CoPs and, therefore, were capable of sustaining conclusions drawn from this example of *post-hoc* theorisation. Their findings and conclusions – reflecting substantial prior fieldwork and as a consequence richer in detail than those of Ng and Pemberton – offer some similar theoretical conclusions, augmented by a more robust empirical warrant. Within these four research groups, key CoP components are identified. Firstly, group identity is constructed in terms of orientation to membership of the group rather than only to the task at hand. Secondly, notions of capacity and talent are framed by group-specific measures and assumptions rather than objective measures of achievement – sometimes leading to tensions between these research CoPs and their host institutions.

Thirdly, the groups share structuring resources to allow for peer learning and – in effect – apprenticeship learning outside formalised patterns of research work. And finally, the research group leaders engage in considerable degrees of work in maintaining both internal relations and relations between the CoP and the institution/wider research community. These practices – which we can clearly identify in terms of maintaining joint enterprise, community relations and brokerage – are characteristic of CoPs. What Degn et al. cannot resolve, of course, is whether or not the external/objective success of these research groups (in terms of funding, publications, esteem and so forth) are a result of their constitution as CoPs or whether their success allows them to emerge/reform as CoPs.

A yet more extensive and richly empirical account is provided by Torres-Purroy and Mas-Alcolea (2022) in their ethnography of two multinational research groups – both in the natural sciences – at a single university in Spain. The fieldwork consisted of an 11-month-long study, generating a consequently rich body of data – field notes, video and audio recordings, documents, photographs and interview transcripts. Drawing on the academic model of CoPs (Wenger, 1998), Torres-Purroy and Mas-Alcolea provide rich descriptions of the three paradigmatic elements of any CoP. In discussing *mutual engagement* within the research groups, they describe the various means by which members come together: group meetings, sharing laboratory space, even informal breaks for coffee. They note that these interactions are role-dependent (more of this work is done by research group leaders than by PhD students, say) and also heterogeneous (different sub-projects involve different people, some meetings are for senior staff only, PhD students had their own activities). The *joint enterprise* of the groups was never made explicit and yet was evident in many interactions, especially group meetings where projects would be discussed. Again, group members had different relationships to the joint enterprise which tended to be established by research group leaders and then conveyed to the other members. Finally, the *shared repertoire* of the research groups is described very much as we might anticipate: scientific objects, books and images, machines and materials, specific uses of language and particular habits – these and others are used to varying degrees by members, depending on status and trajectory. And finally it is worth noting the boundary work done by research group leaders through joining evaluation panels, policy groups, and so forth.

Finally, there are several accounts that focus on how CoPs might help us make sense of researcher development, in terms of specific instances of research work such as academic writing (Murray, 2012), as well as building/encouraging research capacity more widely (Cundill et al., 2015; Hill & Haigh, 2012; Kriner et al., 2015). Murray (2012) contributes to the exploration of communities of research practice through a focus on the more specific notion of a community of writing practice, itself situated within a writing for publication course for academics. Her interest lies in the ways through which the *negotiated identity* of the self as writer can be developed within a community of writers that cuts across academic disciplines. Her participants reported that they had indeed learned much about academic writing practices but were not able to translate these new forms of practice into their own departments/workplaces – a phenomenon that we might explain in terms of boundary crossing and brokerage. Hill and Haigh (2012) are also interested in enhancing research capability, but their study is of a disciplinary cohort – teacher educators – rather than a cross-disciplinary cohort. Here again external drivers contribute to the need for research and for research outputs that are visible and auditable: for the participants in Murray's study (2012), it is the external evaluation of research that provides the backdrop to the 'need' to write and to publish; for the teacher educators, it is an externally-imposed shift in professional identity – namely, that a cohort of staff who did not use to have to be 'research active' now have to be so – that provides the driver. Hill and Haigh (2012) draw on several components of CoP theory in order to describe this shift. Learning to be a researcher through doing *research work* (I shall return to this below) is defined as a form of Legitimate Peripheral Participation, characterised by not only shifts in identity in terms of what it is that teacher educators are expected to do, but also by more formalised structures such as the completion of research qualifications, the provision of mentoring, and help and collaboration in writing research papers and grant applications. Kriner et al. (2015) occupy similar ground, exploring a CoP established within a doctoral programme for students in adult and continuing education as well as higher education. This CoP is presented as a 'learning strategy' to foster scholarly identities. Cundill et al. (2015), by contrast, discuss in some detail what they term *Transdisciplinary* Communities of Practice (TDCoPs) that are self-avowedly heterogeneous not only in terms of the disciplinary backgrounds of the membership but also in terms of the wider networks of practice – academia, government, civic audiences – that they aspire to work with. The two TDCoPs being described speak to vital ecological matters: water resourcing and governance. As such, the focus of the discussion is on brokering and border-crossing: bringing in external stakeholders and promoting knowledge exchange. At the same time, Cundill et al. foreground the work needed to maintain sufficiently harmonious relations between the TDCoPs and the research universities that they are nested in, in a manner similar to that reported by Degn et al. (2018).

Summing Up: Communities of Research Practice

CoP-informed analyses of research work in higher education can and have been used to unpack

- The writing practices of academics.
- The academic development of novice researchers.

- Disciplinary and cross-disciplinary research groups.
- Aspects of the relationships between research groups/clusters and institutional/sector-wide drivers of research activity.

From the standpoint of accounts such as these, how do Communities of Research Practice (CoRPs) come into being? The answer would seem to be contingent on the theoretical stance being taken, the practitioner model tending to inform analyses in terms of more top-down establishment (Cater-Steel et al., 2017), with the academic model focussing on accounts of more organic emergences of CoRPs, insofar as the establishment of these CoRPs is actually addressed. So far so good. What these accounts do not provide, however, is a more detailed account of how 'research work' might actually be constituted within CoP theory. By this I mean to foreground a theoretical problem akin to the pedagogy and assessment problems discussed in earlier chapters: it is clear that the articles discussed above have all positioned research as an aspect of the joint enterprise of the CoPs being described, brought into being through different forms of mutual engagement and requiring both the usage of and contribution to the shared repertoire of the communities. But what is "research work" from a CoP perspective? We can identify where it is and how it is done (within communities, reified in artefacts and routines, enacted through meetings, grant capture and academic publications). Can CoP theory tell us anything about what it actually is?

Research as Work Within Communities of Practice

To the limitations or critiques of CoP theory that we discussed in Chapter 5 we might add questions concerning ways of knowing and reified bodies of knowledge within CoPs. To what extent are CoPs prone to a form of epistemological conservatism, slow to change or to accept innovation (especially when driven by newer rather than older members), and prone to imposing this reluctance to adapt/grow on newly acclimated participants in practice, almost as a condition of their acceptance into the CoP in the first place? The consequence of this confluence of resistance to change and preference for existing ways of doing whatever it is that the community is about, is best summarised by Roberts (2006, pp. 629–630): "communities of practice may become static in terms of their knowledge base and resistant to change". Our problem is that CoP theory is silent when it comes to innovations of any scale, whether these might be relatively small changes in practice or more fundamental shifts in what the community does (Fox, 2000). And yet change is recognised as a fundamental component of any CoP – certainly (and unsurprisingly) not considered by Lave and Wenger (1991) but addressed by Wenger in his later work, firstly in terms of continuities and discontinuities in practice and secondly in terms of evolving forms of mutual engagement (Wenger, 1998, pp. 93–95). And of course, processes of innovation and change are fundamental to the practitioner model (Wenger et al., 2002).

It seems paradoxical to frame CoPs as potentially static in terms of knowledge and knowing when the epistemology of CoP theory more broadly rests on emergence and contingency. Learning and knowing are relational, consequences of ongoing negotiations between members of the community, mediated by the structural and environmental conditions of the community, which itself is prone to influence from other, external communities. Change is a necessary condition of any CoP: practices ebb and flow, boundaries contract and expand, people leave and others join. A CoP, we might propose, is inherently dynamic in both epistemological as well as ontological terms. Mindful of the fact that there are several definitions of what research actually is (and an array of proposals as to how research should be done that is certainly overwhelming to some of us) it nonetheless seems reasonable to use CoP theory to make sense of research as a form of work within a CoP. In so doing, however, I am going to focus very deliberately on articles published within the field of social research broadly and educational research – my own field – specifically: CoP theory is a theory of learning and as such it seems entirely appropriate to focus in this manner and, at the same time, it provides me with as stable a platform on which to base my argument as can be reasonably found (although I shall go on to draw briefly on the broader field of *Science and Technology Studies* in order to be able to make some more widely transferable statements concerning research and knowledge construction).

(Education) Research as a Form of Work

In a paper published twenty years ago (at the time of writing) Phil Hodkinson used CoPs theory to support a broader critique of the then "new orthodoxy" in (education) research, as part of a wider-ranging critique of performativity and audit cultures in higher education (Strathern, 2000). What he labelled then as the new orthodoxy is by now very familiar, and is centred on the establishment of particular methodological orthodoxies in social research, reinforced through the use of published criteria as a means to evaluate and therefore to privilege some forms of educational research whilst downplaying the potentials or insights offered by others. For Hodkinson, the new orthodoxy is summarised as research that is primarily concerned to predict and thereby control educational practice. Notwithstanding the politics of such a managerialist and neoliberal discursive construction, Hodkinson's counter-argument is quite simple: learning is socially constructed and so is knowledge, and research is one of the main ways by which an academic learns something that is new (either to them or to their community) or codifies or reifies a new body of knowledge. Reflecting on his prior – and not uncritical – use of CoP theory (in researching the professional learning of secondary school teachers in England), he posits research as a form of work, resting on a form of learning, situated within CoPs.

Hodkinson (2004) argues that "educational research is a field made up of overlapping communities of practice" (p. 9); it is the learning that is an inextricable element of research work that drives this use of CoPs theory. That is to say, it is through a consideration of how researchers learn to do their research rather than how the social spaces in which research might happen are configured, that he positions research as practice. As such, research work takes on the characteristics of many other forms of work: it can be formal and highly structured, but also messy and informal. It can be learned in part through formal training programmes (attending research methods courses, reading research methods textbooks, and so forth), but also, and equally importantly, through informal practices, rooted in authentic engagement in the research practices of the communities that we join. Novice researchers do their research alongside more experienced colleagues, and learn how to research through authentic engagement with research work through legitimate peripheral participation in communities of research practice. Indeed, it is in how he describes the epistemological nature of research from a CoP standpoint that his critique of the 'new orthodoxy' resides: "... work and learning within the educational research field is...social, cultural and partly tacit ... it follows that research and judgements about research are also social, cultural and embodied" (Hodkinson, 2004, p. 23). The positivist, not to say determinist, discourses of research promulgated by the 'new orthodoxy' are entirely incompatible with an interpretivist stance such as this.

Hodkinson considers the heterogeneity of communities of research practice in a manner similar to Tight (2004): they have particular group identities (adult educators, science educators, feminist researchers, educational psychologists) but are at the same time overlapping, and as researchers we may well join – and therefore learn from – more than one (we can explain this in terms of the *nexus of multimembership*). These communities have their own ways of working – of talking, writing and so forth – and generate their own reifications such as specialist journals. Researchers, and by extension their communities, have different and sometimes competing values, interests, ways of knowing and ways of work: it is entirely unsurprising from a CoP perspective that the work of doing research should therefore be subject to differing – and sometimes contestable – perspectives.

Several aspects of Hodkinson's argument were subsequently addressed by Martyn Hammersley for whom the more significant problem arising from the former's account is to be found in the relationship between educational research, and educational practice (Hammersley, 2005). If CoPs reject institutionalised forms of instruction (as Lave and Wenger proposed) then do they also reject institutionalised research on the basis that the latter rests in some way on forms of institutionalised research training? Does research always have to be indigenous to a community if it is to be linked to authentic and meaningful learning about the practices of that community, and what value might we attach to the knowledge that is created by researchers? Indeed, should these researchers always have to be part of the community being researched? Will the research knowledge produced in a community be practical or practitioner knowledge, or can propositional knowledge or abstract knowledge also be constructed, and if so, can this be translated to other contexts, other communities?

Raising more questions than answers, Hammersley offers, more as points for provocation than as serious attempts to generate conclusions, a series of radical conclusions to the question: should educational research be integrated into CoPs? Subscribing to Lave and Wenger's epistemology, he suggests that a first conclusion might be that the only way educational research can meaningfully inform educational practice is if the two are integrated into a single CoP. Leaning further still into Lave and Wenger (1991), he then proposes that academic research and educational practice can never be integrated due to the rejection of educational discourses and forms in the original iteration of CoP theory. Instead, research would have to focus on the situated learning that is found in "genuine" occupational communities.

Hammersley notes the subsequent shifts in CoP theory that are familiar to us as the academic and practitioner models but do not engage with the possibilities for reconciling CoP theory with formalised educational structures offered by Wenger (1998). But if we consider not only Wenger's consideration of forms of schooling but also the potential of the Learning Architecture, and add to this the resolution of the pedagogy problem outlined earlier, it becomes straightforward to posit the notion of a Community of Pedagogic Practice. As these would be situated across educational sectors (primary, secondary, tertiary) it is then a similarly simple step to either approach these as objects of interest and research from the outside – that is to say, involving brokerage and border crossing – or as in the case of university-based disciplinary communities, to locate research work within the communities as part of their joint enterprise, in the manner that has been outlined above (Degn et al., 2018; Ng & Pemberton, 2013; Torres-Purroy & Mas-Alcolea, 2022).

Some of the arguments raised by Hodkinson and then Hammersley are in turn picked up by Martyn Denscombe within the context of a pragmatist justification for the mixed methods paradigm in social research (that is to say, the use of both quantitative/positivist and qualitative/interpretivist methods). Denscombe (2008) aligns the concept of the CoP with the Kuhnian concept of the research community – a group of people researching at disciplinary as well as at sub-disciplinary levels, through which a research paradigm is operationalised (p. 276). He suggests that one way of thinking about research paradigms is to think about what he terms a *conglomerate* (and what I suspect Wenger would term a *constellation*) of communities of research practice (2008, p. 278) that can be established across different institutions, open at all times to new members just so long as they are committed to the practice of the community (that is, that they work within the same research field), and capable in themselves of changing over time as they respond to new research, to new research findings and to new knowledge. At the heart of this approach is the mixed-methods paradigm, which Denscombe is concerned to posit as a meaningful method/methodological choice for the researcher, notwithstanding the epistemological challenges that it brings. A CoP perspective suits this project because "it is consistent with the pragmatist underpinnings of the approach, through its ability to accommodate the existence of variations and inconsistencies within the approach" (Denscombe, 2008, p. 271). Denscombe carries this pragmatism further, positing CoPs as a lens for inquiry into mixed methods research suitable for those researchers "for whom the distinction between practitioner knowledge and research knowledge is hard to sustain" (Denscombe, 2008: 277). Mapping the characteristics of CoPs onto Kihn's criteria for practice-based research paradigms, Denscombe concludes by suggesting (and categorically not 'demonstrating') that framing CoPs as sites for research allows the choices made about methods to be "in terms of their practical value for dealing with a specific research problem" (Denscombe, 2008, p. 280).

It is worth noting that Denscombe, in laying out his argument, also considers the problem of power within CoPs (Denscombe, 2008, p. 279), alluded to by both Hodkinson and Hammersley but not seriously addressed by either. He suggests that inequalities of power within research communities can be understood as being played out not only inside communities in terms of tension between members of the research community or communities (for example, in the peer review of academic publications) but outside as well in terms of pressures to obtain external funding (for example, pressure to conduct research in particular fields or using specific approaches in order to respond to the requirements of funding agencies or government bodies).

For Denscombe, a CoPs approach is not so much about learning about research work, in contrast to Hodkinson, but about the social life of researchers and the social spaces in which they work, and about the everyday choices that researchers make for primarily practical rather than intellectual reasons. That is to say, Denscombe's focus is on the CoP as the unit of analysis, whereas Hodkinson's focus is on learning about and to do research as legitimate peripheral participation – a learning process that is always situated within a CoP. And finally, as with several of the other authors whose work has been discussed thus far in this chapter, Denscombe draws a series of boundary lines between the practices of the research community and the external factors that, to varying degrees, shape what goes on within these communities and generate differing kinds of boundary practices and examples of border crossings.

Summing Up: Research as Practice Within Communities of Practice

- A critical application of CoP theory allows us to position research as the joint enterprise of a CoP.
- A subscription to CoP theory can be used to inform an approach to research that rests on a sociocultural or social-constructivist perspective; however, this would preclude the adoption of other broadly positivist paradigms. I return to this below.
- Alternatively, a pragmatist approach can be taken that focuses on the practices of the community rather than its epistemological underpinnings.

Interlude: Research as Social, Cultural, and Embodied

Thomas Kuhn's book *The Structure of Scientific Revolutions*, drawn on by Denscombe as discussed above, can be seen as key contribution to the broader field of the development of the study of the history and philosophy of science that in turn contributed to the broader field of Science and Technology Studies (STS). STS, more broadly, and the more specific field of Actor-Network Theory (ANT) have been used to supplement CoPs theory in a number of different ways. Jan Nespor (1994), in his ethnography of undergraduate physics and management studies departments draws on ANT to overcome what he perceives as key deficiencies in the theory of Legitimate Peripheral Participation in CoPs, namely that it cannot answer "the question of how such communities are structured, maintained and connected to one another across space and time" (p. 12). Notwithstanding the later theoretical expansions of Wenger (1998), Nespor's central problematic remains, namely that the focus of inquiry is on the CoP as the unit of analysis with the borders around them and spaces between them regulated to second place. But we might instead argue, following Bruno Latour (one of the architects of ANT) that there are no actual borders or boundaries but merely concentrations of activity that make it look like they are present (Latour, 2013; Tummons, 2021). Steve Fox has also drawn on ANT to resolve perceived deficiencies with CoP theory. As well as approaching the by now well-rehearsed issue of power within CoPs through recourse to an amalgam of ANT and Foucauldian sociology, Fox (2000) uses ANT itself to delve more deeply into the processes of how, at a concrete, step-by-step level, new practices might be acquired within a CoP. To explain this he uses an example from what is arguably a foundational text within ANT by Michel Callon, framing the experts/old-timers within a CoP as forming *obligatory passage points* (Callon, 1984) within the CoP: points in time and space that form necessary encounters for anyone seeking to persuade, or who is to be persuaded, to adopt a particular course of action. ANT is also drawn on by David Barton and Mary Hamilton in their extension of CoP theory more broadly and of reification in particular. For Barton and Hamilton, a consideration of the reifications of any CoP is enriched by ANT, which offers additional theoretical tools "for analysing how reifications travel across time and space to accrue power [and] how social relations are involved in maintaining and promoting (or dismantling) particular reifications" (Barton & Hamilton, 2005, p. 31). ANT, therefore, provides a move away from an individual CoP as our unit of analysis, concentrating instead on the wider fabric of social relations, configured by people and by things that subsume and absorb different, more or less disparate, communities (Swan et al., 2002). It also provides us with ways to think about how human agency can be extended across institutional, geographical and spatial boundaries (Law, 1994). More specifically, ANT leads us to reconsider the qualities and functions of boundary objects, of peripheries, and of brokers and brokerage. For Wenger, these related processes provide a conceptual schema that allows us to theorise the work done at the "edges" of CoPs: as meaning and intention are carried across a constellation, as community members visit some practices and welcome visitors to their own in turn (Wenger, 1998, pp. 106–118). Instead, there might not be such clearly defined boundaries at all (Fox, 2005).

A consideration of ANT as a supplement to CoP theory is, I would argue, worthwhile in and of itself and certainly needs more space than has been devoted to it here (Tummons, 2018). However, the more important consideration is not ANT but STS more broadly. One of the key platforms of STS is the commitment to understanding both technologies and scientific facts as socially constructed – a profound rejection (dismissal, even) of positivist science, although not without controversy (Latour, 1987; Latour & Woolgar, 1986; Sokal & Bricmont, 1999). Irrespective of our stance within what was at the time described as the "science wars", the contribution of STS in particular and of social constructivist epistemologies more broadly (as well as ANT to a lesser extent) to our understanding of research within CoPs is that irrespective of the nature of the Community of Disciplinary Practice within which the research work that we are interested in is situated, the nature of the knowledge being constructed and then reified will always be understood as being socially constructed. And this is why a subscription to CoP theory will always necessitate a rejection of positivist knowledge claims, *unless* a pragmatist stance is adopted.

Universities, Research, and Communities of Practice

With an appropriate theoretical platform in place that allows us to make sense of research as just one kind of practice that might be encompassed by CoP theory, the different issues raised and conclusions drawn by those empirical studies discussed in the first part of this chapter now come into sharper focus: we can apply a *theoretical generalisability* (Gobo, 2008) to the work done by Torres-Purroy and Ma-Alcolea (2021), Murray (2012) and the other works cited, by allowing CP theory to act in not only an explanatory manner but also a predictive one which, we can argue, is – very simply – what any good (social) theory should allow us to do (Gee, 1996; Tight, 2004).

CoP theory allows us to consider research as situated across a diverse range of contexts, as being capable of being made sense of – of negotiated – in a number of ways that will not always be compatible with each but that, crucially, are inherently prone to mutability. CoPs change over time as a consequence of a variety of internal as well as external factors and forces. It follows, therefore, that a Community of Research Practice (or a Community of Disciplinary Practice within which research is just one element of joint enterprise – either formulation will work perfectly well) will also change over time, and therefore the knowledge being constructed and negotiated within that CoP will itself have the potential to be changed as a necessary aspect of its constitution. This might be because the ways that we talk about research (discourse – an element of *mutual engagement*) change; it might be because our equipment and our instruments, or our theories and our materials (all examples of *shared repertoire*); or it might be because the questions that we look to answer and problems that we wish to try to resolve (aspects of *joint enterprise*) change in response to not only our own intellectual experience and learning but also to meet external requirements (for example from funding agencies).

Our research is reified in book chapters and journal articles, posters, websites and PDFs, some intended for a broad academic audience, others for a more specialist audience, and some for non-academic audiences – user groups, policymakers, and professionals. These reifications can travel in many different directions (especially when they are PDFs rather than hard copies) but care needs to be taken when considering how they will be understood when they reach their various destinations. Some texts may need to be accompanied by a person who can act as a literacy sponsor; others may require a high degree of *communicative ability* due to their relatively lack of *transparency*. Many of these texts will only come into being in the first place in order to satisfy the demands of audit and evaluation. Reading them all would be an impossible task, but other reifications – published abstracts, databases, search engines – help us navigate this complex landscape.

The questions that we choose to ask and then answer through our research are generated in several ways. For some of us, it is in our *histories of participation* that dilemmas arise, as we reflect either on specific personal or professional experiences, or on matters of fact or concern that have been presented to us as we have travelled our *trajectories*. For others of us, people from outside our own communities – or constellations of communities – bring narratives and ideas about research with them, either seeking to establish a working relationship at the boundaries of our communities, or hoping to follow a peripheral trajectory as a member of our own CoPs. Theories, concepts, dilemmas and ideas – usually reified within *boundary objects* – can travel to our communities and provoke further thought and research work. At other times, this cross-border traffic of people, concepts, questions an theories will help form, or sustain, communities of research practice that by design operate across an institution or between institutions, either within a single academic discipline or across more than one.

Conclusion: Communities of Research Practice

Research is a form of *work* (Smith, 2005) – a form of practice. Once you know what you are looking for, it is an observable social phenomenon, whether or not it is taking place in a laboratory, an archive, or a (literal or figurative) field. People doing research do things, speak and write in certain ways according to the normative assumptions and/or requirements of their (inter/trans)disciplinary contexts. It makes sense to describe and also interrogate all of these activities, and the material as well as metaphysical resources that sustain them, as well as Communities of Research Practice or as Communities of Disciplinary Practice. In so doing, we can acknowledge the fundamentally contingent nature of what we know, and the importance of making sense of the social contexts within which our ways of knowing are situated, in and through all of the things we do as people working in universities.

References

Barton, D., & Hamilton, M. (2005). Literacy, reification and the dynamics of social interaction. In D. Barton, & K. Tusting (Eds.), *Beyond communities of practice: Language, power and social context* (pp. 14–35). Cambridge University Press.

Callon, M. (1984). Some elements of a sociology of translation: Domestication of the scallops and the fishermen of St Brieuc Bay. *The Sociological Review, 32*(1, supplement), 196–233.

Cater-Steel, A., McDonald, J., Albion, P., & Redmond, P. (2017). Sustaining the momentum: A cross-institutional community of practice for researchers. In J. McDonald, & A. Cater-Steel (Eds.), *Implementing communities of practice in higher education* (pp. 3–17). Springer Nature.

Cundill, G., Roux, D., & Parker, J. (2015). Nurturing communities of practice for transdisciplinary research. *Ecology and Society, 20*(2), 22.

Degn, L., Franssen, T., Sørensen, M., & de Rijcke, S. (2018). Research groups as communities of practice: A case study of four high-performing research groups. *Higher Education, 76*(2), 231–246.

Denscombe, M. (2008). Communities of practice: A research paradigm for the mixed methods approach. *Journal of Mixed Methods Research, 2*(3), 270–283.

Fox, S. (2000). Communities of practice, foucault and actor-network theory. *Journal of Management Studies, 37*(6), 853–867.

Fox, S. (2005). An actor-network critique of community in higher education: Implications for networked learning. *Studies in Higher Education, 30*(1), 95–110.

Gee, J. P. (1996). *Social linguistics and literacies: Ideology in discourses* (2nd ed.). RoutledgeFalmer.

Gobo, G. (2008). Reconceptualising generalisation: Old issues in a new frame. In A. Alasuutari, L. Bickman, & J. Brannen (Eds.), *The Sage Handbook of social research methods* (pp. 193–213). Sage.

Hammersley, M. (2005). What can the literature on communities of practice tell us about educational research? Reflections on some recent proposals. *International Journal of Research and Method in Education, 28*(1), 5–29.

Hill, M., & Haigh, M. (2012). Creating a culture of research in teacher education: Learning research within communities of practice. *Studies in Higher Education*, *37*(8), 971–988.

Hodkinson, P. (2004). Research as a form of work: Expertise, community and methodological objectivity. *British Educational Research Journal*, *30*(1), 9–26.

Kriner, B., Coffman, K., Adkisson, A., Putman, P., & Monaghan, C. (2015). From students to scholars: The transformative power of communities of practice. *Adult Learning*, *26*(2), 73–80.

Latour, B. (1987). *Science in action*. Harvard University Press.

Latour, B. (2013). *An inquiry into modes of existence*. Transl. C Porter. Harvard University Press.

Latour, B., & Woolgar, S. (1986). *Laboratory life: The construction of scientific facts (2nd ed.)*. Princeton University Press.

Lave, J., & Wenger, E. (1991). *Situated learning: Legitimate peripheral participation*. Cambridge University Press.

Law, J. (1994). *Organising modernity*. Blackwell.

Murray, R. (2012). Developing a community of research practice. *British Educational Research Journal*, *38*(5), 783–800.

Nespor, J. (1994). *Knowledge in motion: Space, time and curriculum in undergraduate physics and management*. RoutledgeFalmer.

Ng, L., & Pemberton, J. (2013). Research-based communities of practice in UK higher education. *Studies in Higher Education*, *38*(10), 1522–1539.

Roberts, J. (2006). Limits to communities of practice. *Journal of Management Studies*, *43*(3), 623–637.

Smith, D. (2005). *Institutional ethnography: A sociology for people*. Altamira Press.

Sokal, A., & Bricmont, J. (1999). *Fashionable nonsense: Postmodern intellectuals' abuse of science*. St. Martin's Press.

Strathern, M. (Ed.) (2000). *Audit cultures: Anthropological studies in accountability, ethics and the academy*. Routledge.

Swan, J., Scarbrough, H., & Robertson, M. (2002). The construction of communities of practice in the management of innovation. *Management Learning*, *33*(4), 477–496.

Tight, M. (2004). Research into higher education: An a-theoretical community of practice? *Higher Education Research and Development*, *23*(4), 395–411.

Tight, M. (2013). Discipline and methodology in higher education research. *Higher Education Research and Development*, *32*(1), 136–151.

Tight, M. (2014). Discipline and theory in higher education research. *Research Papers in Education*, *29*(1), 93–110.

Tight, M. (2015). Theory application in higher education research: The case of communities of practice. *European Journal of Higher Education*, *5*(2), 111–126.

Tight, M. (2018). *Higher education research: The developing field*. Bloomsbury.

Torres-Purroy, H., & Mas-Alcolea, S. (2021). Applying the community of practice theory in higher education: The case of the research group. In M. Tight, & J. Huisman (Eds.), *Theory and method in higher education research* (Vol. 7, pp. 39–53). Emerald.

Tummons, J. (2018). *Learning architectures in higher education: Beyond communities of practice*. Bloomsbury.

Tummons, J. (2021). Ontological pluralism, modes of existence, and actor-network theory: Upgrading latour with latour. *Social Epistemology*, *35*(1), 1–11.

Wenger, E. (1998). *Communities of practice: Learning, meaning and identity*. Cambridge University Press.

Wenger, E., McDermott, R., & Snyder, W. (2002). *Cultivating communities of practice*. Harvard Business School Press.

Index

Actor-Network Theory 92, 124
Adult Math Project 19–20
agency 74–75, 125
agentic individual 74
alignment 9, 46, 101, 107; and assessment 106, 110; between communities of practice 55, 93
artefacts 57, 60, 64, 70, 90, 92; histories of 14; maintenance of 103; *see also* reification
assessment 13, 99; authenticity 109–111; in a community of practice 102–103, 109; criteria 107; problem 100, 108; reification of 24; reliability 112; as social practice 101–102; validity 110–111
authenticity 53–54, 65

boundaries 28, 40–41, 45, 73; coincident 91, 100; formation 86–87
boundary crossing 60, 86, 88, 96
boundary encounter 86, 89
boundary object 86, 90–92
boundary work 97, 117
brokers 89, 94–96
brokerage 107, 117, 122, 125
brokering 89–90, 111

communicative ability 104–105, 126
Community of Practice (CoP) 2–3; academic and practitioner models of 4–5, 8–9, 36; change in 26–28, 31; curriculum and 14, 40, 63–64, 85, 99, 101; elements of 6–8, 11–15; history of 4–5; interdisciplinary 41; learning in 22–25; virtual 87
constellation 30, 37, 70, 94–96
curriculum 13, 20–21; professional 29

discourse 14–15, 33, 39, 41, 53, 72, 126

gender 7, 72–74

identity 39, 60–61, 73–76, 93–94
illegitimate peripheral participation 68–69
individual 74–76
inter-generational encounters 72, 77

joint enterprise 6–7, 12–13, 23, 32, 40

language 71–72, 117
learning architecture 55–56, 103; conceptual foundations of 58–62; design of 63–64
legitimate peripheral participation (LPP) 22–24, 53–55, 102
literacy 72, 92, 107, 126

membership 28, 54, 70
multimembership 28, 39, 92–96, 121
mutual engagement 6, 9–12, 24, 32, 40, 58, 94, 117, 119, 126

negotiation of meaning 44, 71, 105–106

old-timers 12, 22–23, 27, 39, 53, 61, 72, 108, 111; power of, 77

participation 22–23, 25–28, 42, 44, 57–58, 61–62, 70, 75; assessment and 103–105; co-participation 74; new forms of 90
pedagogy 5, 23, 52–53, 73, 108–109; pedagogy problem 54, 99–100
power 60, 71, 77–78, 95, 123, 124–125
professional practice 85–86

qualifications 25, 85, 89, 118

reconciliation work 88, 93, 99
reification 42, 57–58, 124–125; assessment and 103–105; text-based 104
research 115–118; in CoPs 119–123

shared repertoire 7–8, 14–15, 24–26, 32; and assessment 108–109; and boundary objects 90–91; and discourse 72, 106; and teaching 62
situated learning 8, 24, 53–54, 99, 102, 111; and assessment 108; and research 122

social justice 29
social practice, 21, 73, 75; cognition as 3; teaching as 62
structuring resources 59, 62–63, 111, 117

teaching 46–49, 62–63, 94–95, 99
textual artefacts 30, 85, 107; and assessment 104
trajectories 26–29; 85, 88, 92, 103, 126
transparency 104, 107, 126

virtual learning environment 45–47, 101
visitors 56, 92, 95, 96, 125

For Product Safety Concerns and Information please contact our EU
representative GPSR@taylorandfrancis.com
Taylor & Francis Verlag GmbH, Kaufingerstraße 24, 80331 München, Germany

www.ingramcontent.com/pod-product-compliance
Lightning Source LLC
Chambersburg PA
CBHW070316240426
43661CB00057B/2669